In memory of
Robert Cupitt
(1911–1992)
and
Norah Cupitt
(1913–1997)

Mysticism After Modernity

Don Cupitt

BLACKWELL
Publishers

First published 1998

Transferred to digital print 2004

2 4 6 8 10 9 7 5 3 1

Blackwell Publishers Inc.
350 Main Street
Malden, Massachusetts 02148
USA

Blackwell Publishers Ltd
108 Cowley Road
Oxford OX4 1JF
UK

Library of Congress Cataloging-in-Publication Data
Cupitt, Don.
  Mysticism after modernity / Don Cupitt.
    p.   cm.
  Includes bibliographical references and index.
  ISBN 0–631–20763–5 (hardcover : alk. paper). —
ISBN 0–631–20764–3 (pbk. : alk. paper)
    1. Mysticism.   2. Deconstruction.   3. Postmodernism—Religious
aspects—Christianity.   I. Title.
BV5083.C87   1997
291.4'22—dc   21 97–11925
                CIP

British Library Cataloguing in Publication Data
A CIP catalogue record for this book is available from the
British Library.

Typeset in 10½/13 pt Meridien
by Graphicraft Typesetters Ltd, Hong Kong
Printed and bound in Great Britain by Marston Book Services Limited, Oxford

This book is printed on acid-free paper

contents

the mysticism of

secondariness

Opinions may differ about just when it was that the Modern age suddenly confronted its own deepest assumptions and found itself compelled to recognize that it didn't actually believe in them any more, but perhaps the best candidate is the year 1968, a turbulent time in Prague, Paris and Chicago. Since then we have increasingly thought of ourselves as living in a "postmodern" period – a term that we use not by way of signifying that we have successfully completed the transition to a new understanding of the human condition, but rather by way of admitting that as yet we *haven't*. We have a name for what is gone, but not for what is coming. We have lost an old worldview, but we do not yet see very clearly what will replace it. We do see that our new leaders are stripping out all the old content from liberalism, socialism, and the other typically Modern faiths. "New Labour," for example, is the Labour Party *minus* socialism. American politics, one gathers, is now politics *minus* politics; politics as a charm offensive. The new university is the university *minus* both the traditional and the liberal conceptions of what a university was supposed to be and to do. And so on – but what exactly is coming in to replace the old faiths and institutions? That is harder to say.

One way to get clearer is to study what is happening to religion after modernity. In the past, all of people's ideas about reality and objectivity – their sense of life's basic *shape* – depended ultimately upon the authority of a deeply ingrained sense of religious law, and proximately upon a framework of shared philosophical assumptions. In modernity these assumptions especially concerned the human subject, consciousness, experience, reason, and language. But in postmodern times they have all broken down. Metaphysical realism has come to an end, and our whole world-view has become very much more pluralized, pragmatic, free-floating, and maintained by continual *bricolage*, or improvisation. In theological terms, this adds up (says Mark C. Taylor, in a very influential book)[1] to the Death of God, the Disappearance of the Self, the End of History, and the Closure of the Book; the end therefore of all forms of realism and supernaturalism; the end of objective Truth, and of all forms of faith in some future and hoped-for totalization of the human world.

All this was intensively discussed in the theology of the 1980s. The debates were useful, if only because they reminded us that when we are in a period of transition between one great cultural epoch and another, the best available vocabulary for describing what is happening is still that of theology. For theology – and especially *Christian* theology – actually arose as a subject out of just such a background. It was born seeking to articulate and to diffuse the conviction that a radical change of dispensation had occurred, and a new epoch had begun. It is then not surprising that in our own time the various prophets of postmodernity, in philosophy from Nietzsche to the early Derrida, and in theology from Albert Schweitzer to Thomas J.J. Altizer, should have drawn so heavily upon the language of theology, and especially apocalyptic theology, to communicate their messages.

A decade ago, the conclusion that some of us drew from all this was that from now on we must take a "consistently mythological" view of religious belief. All religious belief, including belief in God and life after death, is mythological. Henceforth religious doctrine should be seen simply as providing us with a language to live by, and a set of model narratives for us to draw upon in building our own life-stories. One name coined to describe this position was "active non-realism," meaning: "If you really want it all to be true, then it is entirely up to you to *make* it all true, in your own way and in your own life!" A religious faith is a project; we can make it all come true by the way we execute it.

The next step in clarifying what postmodernity is becoming will be to explain the new postmodern type of religious experience, now becoming available to us. I call this the mysticism of secondariness. It is a form of religious consciousness that actively rejoices in and affirms all the features of the postmodern condition that most shock and alarm the surviving Old Guard of the Enlightenment.[2] It may seem at first sight to be a complete reversal of the older kind of mysticism, but I am going to argue that classical mysticism was itself already a subversive and transgressive kind of writing, and that our new postmodern mysticism can be seen as a continuation and a radicalization of the older tradition.

The key to understanding classical mysticism, I shall argue, lies in the religious background out of which it arises. Our great "world religions" are (broadly speaking) religions of personal salvation. Each individual adherent was originally promised a share – indeed, an *equal* share – in religious happiness. But as time went on and the faiths became institutionalized, control of the community everywhere fell into the hands of a ruling group of religious professionals. Priests, scribes, interpreters, and lawyers, they guarded tradition and monopolized control of the sacred text, worship, doctrine, preaching, and religious law. The religious life of the individual was now lived in subjection to a large and bureaucratic salvation-machine, and personal experience of the highest religious happiness was deferred to the heavenly world after death. Thus a faith-tradition that had originally delivered personal liberation now delivered only a condition of extreme religious alienation, and so it remains to this day.

Against this background, the writers commonly called "mystics" were usually (though not quite always) persons of low ecclesiastical rank, from the inferior clergy, the religious, and the laity. They included relatively large numbers of townspeople, of women, and of poets. In their devotional writings they are conspicuously silent about the great salvation-machine and all its concerns. Recalling the older charismatic and more democratic tradition, they try to write their way and ours to a condition of personal religious happiness.

However, such writing is very dangerous. The religious authorities are always very alert, and quick to detect an implicit

criticism of themselves and a threat to their power and priv-
ileges. The mystical writer faces a suspicion of heresy and a
threat of persecution, often with the utmost severity. It is therefore necessary to write in a special code and to maintain what
is called in Washington – as I understand – "plausible deniability."
So the mystic will often start from an innocuous-sounding and
entirely traditional theme or doctrine. Only as the argument
develops does one begin to suspect that some kind of subversive
or deconstructive commentary is being written.

The mystic *has* to be a deconstructor, because religious orthodoxies were all constructed with the aim of making final religious happiness (or salvation, or the Vision of God) impossible
in this life. Orthodoxy tries to prove to the individual that
because we cannot personally attain complete religious happiness we must be content to be faithful and obedient children
living in trustful dependence upon the salvation-machine. In
this context, the mystic was compelled to deconstruct orthodoxy, and especially the standard doctrine of God, if she was to
achieve personal religious happiness. But if she was found out,
she got burnt.

The fierce persecution of mystics by their own co-religionists
has been a characteristic mainly of the Jewish, Muslim, and
Christian traditions. In these traditions of prophetic monotheism, a strong doctrine of revelation led to the rise of a body of
religious professionals who claimed to be the sole authorized
interpreters of revelation and guardians of orthodoxy. The religious authorities control truth and see themselves as having a
clear duty to put down error.

The Eastern history has of course been rather different; but
the oriental traditions have also known the institutionalization
of religion and the rise of a religious rhetoric that seems to put
final "release" thousands of lifetimes away. Against that kind of
background, some Eastern mystical movements – Hindu Bhakti,
Amida Buddhism, etc. – were clearly attempts to show the
ordinary person that it is possible to bypass the temple, the
system, and the professionals, and to seize religious happiness
for yourself. And to do so very quickly, if you are wholehearted
enough.

In Buddhism, however, mysticism is also much more than a protest movement. It is constitutive of the whole tradition, and in a very special way. The principal cause of humanity's prevalent unhappiness is held to be a false construction of the world. A few of us may seek a cure by studying Buddhist philosophy, and all of us can find therapy by diligent practice. Just sitting in meditation, if we persist long enough, will gradually relax us and dissolve away the false dualisms and the ideas of substance that were troubling us. The more everything – including the self – is melted down into a silent outpouring of pure insubstantial secondariness (I call this "the Fountain"), the happier we get to be. To our own considerable surprise, we find ourselves unlearning our way down to the most perfect happiness in the purest Emptiness.

In the Western and monotheistic traditions it is usually felt to be a matter of duty that one should hold to very "realistic" ideas both of God, and of the created world. People then tend to perceive the mystic as a seer who has special insight into questions of metaphysics. He has a special esoteric knowledge of superfacts. He rests in the knowledge of what is absolutely Real; and *that* is the state we should aim for. As a result, most people overlook the very strong negative and therapeutic element in Western mysticism. It too has a strand that talks about *un*knowing, about learned ignorance and about Negative Theology. And all this negative talk has, I shall argue, a deliberately subversive intent.

All this was obscured in the period 1790–1970, when our Modern conception of mysticism was developed. The mystics were then repackaged as psychic sensitives who had wonderful, wonderful experiences that confirmed the truth of orthodoxy! One of the aims of this present essay is to point out the great injustice that was done to the mystics when they were thus "rehabilitated" as orthodox. They were being canonized in retrospect by the same System that had persecuted them.

Their posthumous rehabilitation did the mystics no good at all, and greatly confused the definition of mysticism. There was an ancient tradition of apologetic argument from a supernatural occurrence back to a supernatural cause of it. Now it was being suggested that "mystical experiences" were comparable with fulfilled prophecies and miracles: they too were supernatural events within the soul that must have been caused by God. If so, the more supernatural the better; and, as a result, a variety of highly eccentric characters who had experienced ecstasies, performed miracles, heard voices, and seen visions came to be classed as "mystics," along with subtle writers such as the pseudo-Dionysius and Eckhart.

The result was, and still is, an intellectual mess. Here we are concerned with the hard-core literary mystics, writers who stand in the tradition of neoplatonism and the Negative Theology. These writers play curious games with religious language, exploiting its paradoxes and tensions in ways that seem very often to enrage the authorities. We need to understand what these writers were doing, and why they were perceived as being so deadly dangerous.

There is a further point: because mystical writing, especially in the hands of a very great figure such as Eckhart, tends to deconstruct the official Church ontology, it may be seen as anticipating more recent styles of deconstructive criticism and radical theology. And if even classical mysticism was already tending to undermine metaphysics, and was already tending to find religious happiness by reducing everything to secondariness, then I can claim that our postmodern mysticism of secondariness is the true continuator of the older tradition.

I should here briefly introduce the special use in philosophy of the terms "primary" and "secondary." In his *Topics* c.5 Aristotle makes a distinction between primary and secondary substances, saying that individual men and horses are examples of primary substances, and that the universal kinds "man" and "horse" are secondary substances. In fact, he's attacking Plato. Plato put the universal first and the singular second, whereas Aristotle puts the particular individuals first and regards the general word as secondary. It's a universal term, an abstraction, a construct.

Margaret Thatcher, as everyone knows, once said something very Aristotelian about the individual and society. When she said that "there is no such thing as society: there are only individuals and their families," she surely meant that in her view political thought should begin from the individual as primary, and treat society as a secondary construct.

However, our immediate point is that both Plato and Aristotle are agreed on the claim that *something* is primary, and that we should begin with it; whereas non-realism and the mysticism of secondariness take a novel and different view, the view that *nothing* is primary. There is no specially privileged and secure starting-point, first principle or foundation from which to start.

Consider, for example, the mind–body problem. If you begin from a standpoint within human consciousness, you will take the mind as given, and the existence of the external and supposedly independent material world will appear problematic. If, on the other hand, you begin as many scientists do from an objective standpoint and take the existence of a world of material bodies as given, you will regard mind as problematic, and wonder how some material bodies have managed to become conscious. Now, nothing gives us any objective guarantee that one of these starting-points is correct and the other mistaken. The only criterion for choosing between them is, perhaps, pragmatic. We should use, on each occasion, the one that works best and gives us the best overall picture.

Is there any other possibility? I have myself suggested a third view: why not start from the movement of language, picturing it as moving along the frontier between the mind and the world? Then we can treat the material world as a construct on the outer surface of language, and the world of mind as a construct on the inner surface of language. Surely that will lead to a better and more complete picture than is given by either idealism or materialism?

I hold that it does; but I have to confess that even language may not give us a rock-solid starting-point. It too is secondary. It too can be seen as a mere construct. We made it up. So, when all proposed foundations or fixed starting-points have failed, we find ourselves obliged to admit that everything is secondary. There is no pure datum, no primary substance, no "absolute," nothing that is always ontologically prior. Nothing is always real, from every point of view. We are always in secondariness, moving around as a sniper does, trying different angles. We must give up the old mythological idea of a complete account of reality from Beginning to End. We never come to any Absolute Beginning, nor to any Last End.

In that case the kind of religion, and the kind of mysticism, that sought for something that is eternally primary is out-of-date. We need to attempt a quite novel approach.

The mysticism of secondariness, then, is thoroughgoing and free-floating relativism embraced with rapturous joy. The older "platonic" kind of mysticism was usually claimed to be *noetic*[3] – by which I mean that people saw religious experience as a special supernatural way of knowing something Higher that was itself correspondingly super-natural. Religion was associated with philosophical rationalism and a two-worlds cosmology. In religious experience you distanced yourself from the senses and this world and stilled your mind, in order to attend to the unchanging, non-sensuous divine things of a higher world. It seemed obvious to people that in order to be completely happy we must turn our minds away from the Many to the One, from the changing world to the unchangeable things of the spirit, and from mediated, secondary, or discursive thinking to immediate and intuitive vision of something ultimate and primary. But now, with the end of metaphysics and two-worlds dualism, we should give up the idea that mystical consciousness is noetic. That is, we give up the idea that mysticism is a special wordless way of intuitively knowing the things of another and higher world. We may discover that we no longer wish to go *beyond*. We do not hunger for "absolutes," and we are happy to give up the whole idea of equating blessedness with the gaining of a higher kind of knowledge. It is possible to be completely happy without either absolute knowledge or absolute Reality. The mysticism of secondariness is mysticism *minus* metaphysics, mysticism *minus* any claim to special or privileged knowledge, and mysticism without any other world than this one. We now get – you get, and I get – that feeling of eternal happiness, not by contrast with, but *directly off* everything that is merely relative, secondary, derived, transient, sensuous, and only-skin-deep. We have quite forgotten the old hunger for what is basic, rock-solid, certain, and unchangeable: we are content with fluidity and mortality. We very much like the fact that linguistic meanings are so imprecise, mobile, and constantly shifting, because it makes writing possible. We even like the transitoriness of our values, because it obliges us constantly to be reimagining our values, reaffirming them, and falling in love with them afresh. One of the most important philosophical insights that has precipitated us into postmodernity is the discovery that because we never come to any absolute beginning or last end, nothing is absolute or primary, nor even wholly independent. We are always in the midst of things, and everything is secondary. Everything becomes, and everything passes away. Relativism should not be a bogey to us: it is true, and religiously speaking it is good news. Nothing is substantial, everything is dependent and interrelated: and why not? Why shouldn't we just give up the idea that there's something *wrong* with being secondary and fleeting?

A simple, even hackneyed, image of a world in which everything is secondary: imagine a summer idyll in which you are drifting down river, lying in a flat-bottomed boat. Sunlight dancing on the water is reflected up onto the undersides of the overhanging willows that line the banks, creating flickering, dappled patterns. Seeing the trees thus brightly lit from below as you lie back and drift beneath them breaks you out of your normal habit of seeing the world as four-square and solidly grounded, dark below and light above. Gravity is almost reversed. Dreamily, you see everything, yourself included, as rocking, floating, insubstantial, and only-an-effect. Everything is "phenomenal," literally a-shining and a-seeming. And this is blissful! You feel no inclination to condemn it as a mere shadowplay. On the contrary, the phenomenalist vision of the world is itself also a religious vision: it has cropped up as such in the Indian tradition, as well as in the West's empiricist philosophy and late-Impressionist painting.

Now this, it must be emphasized, is only an *image* of the mysticism of secondariness, and not quite an *instance* of it. The mysticism of secondariness is not a form of nature-mysticism, such as is familiar in writers like W.D. Hudson and Richard

Jefferies. In postmodernity culture precedes nature, so that the featherlight dancing world of relativities that we are always already immersed in is the world of linguistic *meaning*, which houses and enfolds the world of empirical fact.

In a well-known remark the young Wittgenstein declared that it is not the way the world is that is mystical, but the fact *that* it is.[4] Wrong: what is mystical is the way the strange magical world of symbolic meanings holds the common world, the world of human life, in the hollow of its hand.

In this book I shall attempt to explain the mysticism of secondariness by considering how it has arisen out of the older tradition – a program that gives rise to a special literary difficulty. It was perhaps St Paul who entrenched in our Western tradition the paradoxical idea of ineffable truth, or knowledge beyond words (II *Corinthians* 12:4). *Arrēta rēmata*, unsaid sayings, unspeakable speech, is his phrase. He forgets that in describing the indescribable as indescribable he *is* describing it.

Similarly, Augustine, in a passage to be discussed later, is quite confident that he can soar beyond language, beyond the world and beyond even his own mind. Momentarily, he tells us, he touches the Eternal, and then he falls back into language – not noticing that he never left it! (*Confessions* IX, c.X, 24; and below, p. 70).

In the Buddhist tradition it has long been recognized that the idea of a truth beyond words is too paradoxical to be self-consistently stated. But the Western tradition has been relatively naive, and (for special historical reasons, to be explained) the type of thinking that I call Modern has kept going the idea that there can be extra-linguistic experience, knowledge and truth, right up to the present day. Indeed, we have here a crucially important difference between modernity and postmodernity. When a Modern reads a mystical text, he seems to understand *realistically* all the talk about experience, a spiritual world, the Unitive State, timelessness, immediate knowledge, and so on. When a Postmodern reads the same text, she reads it as a literary construct produced within a literary tradition. In Margaret Thatcher's sense, "there is no such thing" as experience: mysticism is a kind of writing and we do not need to invoke "experience" in order to explain it, when its literary pedigree is so easy to trace. Most people, surely, recognize that Dante's *Divine Comedy* is not a straightforward travel book, but an epic poem. So, if in the case of Dante we do not think of the poet as claiming to have enjoyed special supernatural experiences, why should we not learn to read John of the Cross and the other great mystics in the same way?

A postmodern person would prefer never to write as if we may first have cognitive experience of something, and then only at a later stage tackle the problem of how to put it into words. Language goes all the way down; there is no meaningfulness and no cognition prior to language. But because in the present book I am trying to write the transition from a late-Modern to a fully postmodern understanding of religious experience and mysticism, I do at times use language that can be read in the Modern way.

Grateful thanks to Steven Shakespeare for criticisms, and to Linda Allen for word-processing my many revisions of this text.

D.C.
Cambridge, 1997

the modern construction of mysticism and religious experience

Everything comes to be and passes away; everything has a history. And that includes "experience," "religious experience," "mysticism," and "spirituality." We invented all these things, and did so rather more recently than you may imagine. If you doubt this, then produce an ancient or medieval use of one of these terms in something like its contemporary sense. In fact, our current ways of using them all were developed during the Modern period, and they still carry a heavy freight of modernist ideology. Until recently this was to their advantage, but now with the breakdown of many or all of the deep assumptions of modernity their stock has suddenly slumped. They are in difficulties, and they need to be refurbished.

The story commonly told about all this runs as follows: modernity, beginning in the sixteenth and seventeenth centuries (or maybe somewhat earlier, in the later Middle Ages), set out to see everything from the viewpoint of the individual human subject. The touchstone of truth was relocated within human subjectivity. Everything was to be reconstructed around the subject and redescribed in terms of the way it looks to the individual to whom it presents itself, who appropriates it and puts it to use in life. In philosophy, one typical beginning was with the *cogito*, "I think, therefore I am," of René Descartes in 1637: in religion, the individual typically sought personal assurance of salvation by a personal act of faith. Thus Luther, near the beginning of modernity, demands that we must personally appropriate each clause of the Creed by putting after it the phrase *pro me*, on my behalf, for me; and he thereby sets in motion a process of internalization, by which the old objective framework of dogma is progressively ingested and absorbed into the religious life and experience of the individual. Verified subjectively and within the believer's own life, liberal Protestant faith becomes all the more effective and dynamic as it is emancipated from the old dependence upon the external authority of the Church. When it has become true in me and for me, I can act *upon* it, and live it out.

During the next two centuries or so a similar shift to a more anthropocentric and activist outlook takes place in many areas of the culture. In world-view there is a move away from the old dogmatic natural philosophy to the new rapidly developing experimental sciences of nature. Politics begins to move from absolute monarchy towards liberal democracy. Faith in the possibility, even the inevitability, of progressive and final human liberation grows ever stronger. A certain consumerism begins to affect the way people speak about religion, art, morality, and, of course, economics. The self seems to become ever bigger and more demanding. It begins to overreach itself. It makes everything else instrumental to its own needs: it sucks the world dry. Its confidence becomes so great that it recklessly directs its own greedy, reductive, exploitative ways of knowing even against itself. The violent paradoxes that result cause it to crash.[1] The result is postmodernism and the dissolution of the subject. A certain kind of optimistic humanism has come to an end. Thereafter, there are two options, one of which seems to favour the prefix neo- (e.g., neo-orthodoxy, neo-conservatism), while the other prefers a multitude of coinages beginning with post-. Right postmodernism has throughout the twentieth century been attempting in one way or another to restore traditional authority both in politics and in religion. The other option, left postmodernism, is explored in this book.

Against this background we can now see what has been happening to *experience, religious experience, mysticism,* and *spirituality*.

During the Modern period, they all got swept up into the excitement of the Modern project and were redescribed in terms of the contribution they could make to the ever-greater enrichment and fulfilment of the self. To reach its fullest development, the self must be fed with a properly balanced diet of aesthetic experience, moral experience, religious experience, and so on, so that it can grow really *big* (and we note that educationists designing school syllabuses still actually talk like this). If everyone's life-task is to grow a large, mature, and well-rounded self, then certainly religion needs to be on the menu, and the true gourmet of selfhood will wish to study the mystics too.

The last of these epicures of selfhood and connoisseurs of mysticism were still writing as late as the 1960s. I shall charitably refrain from naming them. It is kinder to leave them in obscurity because their deep assumption, that to be endlessly preoccupied with developing and enriching the self is both very interesting and highly religious, now exposes them to ridicule. (Is it *always* the case that whenever the hidden assumptions that underlie a vision of the good life are made explicit, they look utterly foolish?)

Maybe all this is enough to explain why the ideas about *experience, religious experience,* and *mysticism* which developed and flourished in the Modern period are suddenly in difficulties; but I also have some further and interesting complications to point out. The older theological and philosophical outlook was hugely powerful and difficult to overthrow. In order to subvert it, modernity (especially in the person of René Descartes) borrowed certain themes from it and turned them back against it. This strategy, however, left modernity with internal paradoxes and tensions that were eventually to prove its downfall. Indeed, the best argument for right postmodernism will be a proof that the great tradition of Objective Rationalism (or "metaphysics," or capital-P Philosophy) cannot be successfully subverted without leaving the one who subverts it fatally wounded by internal paradoxes. This means we have no choice but to be sceptical neo-conservatives. Our own reply here to this fearsome argument will consist simply of an attempt to express a left postmodernist religious outlook that is free from such internal paradoxes, and therefore not terminally sick at its birth.

We proceed briefly to consider experience, religious experience, mysticism, and spirituality in turn.

Experience

Although I have described the Modern outlook as being very active in temper, the typically Modern use of the word "experience," still generally current, is notably *passive*. Experiences are the opposite of actions: they are all the things that we register as happening to us, rather than the things that we do. What I experience is what I have lived through, passed through, undergone, endured or enjoyed, observed or felt. I am conscious of, or aware of my experiences as impressing themselves or impinging upon my sensibility, and so becoming part of the stream of my mental history and in due course being added to my stock of memories.

Here we seem to differ remarkably from the people of antiquity. In those days, a human life was seen as a chain of *actions*. If you looked back on a life and praised it, you praised it as a series of noble deeds. The point was that in a noble deed one saw a momentary disclosure of the eternal in time. But nowadays people's view of their own past lives seems to consist entirely of memories of their experiences. Tourists, holidaymakers, and others are not *doing* anything very much: they are simply purchasing and laying down stocks of pleasant memories to be replayed and enjoyed in their later years. People are not agents any longer; they are the consumers and the recorders of their own experience. They are their own video-librarians, collecting and arranging shelves of happy memories.

Until the seventeenth century, though, the term "experience" did have a predominantly active meaning. The Latin verb *experiri* meant "to put to the test, to try out." So the Jacobean dramatist James Shirley has a character saying, "Make Experience of my loyalty, by some service," meaning simply: "Try me." Experience was active. It was trial, test, proof, or demonstration; and the old Latin tag *Experientia docet*, experience teaches, meant that we should learn, not by lying back and letting life happen to us, but rather by actively trying out who and what can be relied upon. In this old and active use, *experience* (verb and noun) overlapped considerably with *experiment* (verb and noun), which came from the same root.

In which case, why is it that experience has since the seventeenth century become so very passive? The answer is obvious. In religion, in philosophy, and in science alike, early Modern writers are very keen indeed to persuade us that purely given and passively registered personal experience can be a clean and uncontaminated source of new and very valuable knowledge.[2] Objective truth can be certified to each individual within the sphere of his or her own subjectivity. In principle, at least, each individual is capable of gaining objective knowledge, all by himself. For this to work, the self has to be seen as the disengaged, impartial accumulator of an incoming stream of clean data from outside, about which it theorizes. The knowledge that we gather is thus seen as being most objective when our relation to life is most passive. Strangely, modernist confidence and activism grew out of a completely passive starting-point.

Why? Because in medieval times in particular the dominant regime of truth had been so very objective. There was just one final Truth of things, out-there in the mind of God. God had predetermined and would in the end publish and establish all truth, the whole Truth. Meanwhile the Church had an exclusive franchise: it effectively controlled all communication between God and humans.

The whole system was indeed a form of Objective Rationalism. It meant reason out-there, meanings fixed out-there, Truth ready-made out-there, a complete ready-made predesigned Cosmos out-there with its entire history preplanned from Creation to Judgement. How could dissenters get any leverage against such a grandiose and total truth-power? There seemed to be no scope for the humble individual either to change any meanings or to construct any new truth. The individual was too weak. Every genuine thinker is a kind of artist who feels impelled to build a world; but in the context of later medieval theology such a person is excluded *a priori* as a blasphemer. As happens today in some Muslim countries – and elsewhere, I might add – the creative person was made to feel wicked all the way down, an abomination, someone who has no right to exist.

How could one get any leverage: where could one insert wedges and open up cracks in the system? There are various familiar strategies, scholarly, artistic, and literary. One might examine the system's historical and philosophical claims, one could comment upon it in various oblique and ironical ways, and, best of all, one could like the oriental wrestler throw it by turning its own strength against itself.

It is this background that explains the force, and the sheer cunning, of the appeal to passive experience. The old religious cosmology was extremely realistic, in the philosophical sense. It held that the world is already out-there and fully formed by God, prior to any apprehension or description or theorizing of it by us. We've already got a complete and ready-made world laid on for us by God, and we were predesigned to fit into it. *But in that case we can trust our senses and our cognitive faculties: we can exploit the world's ready-madeness in order to build our own system of objective knowledge of it!* God in his goodness has put us in a situation in which we can find out the truth by ourselves, autonomously, and without having to depend upon religious authority. Instead of receiving truth after repentance and submission, we can see it directly by the light of reason. All we need to do is to carry out a thorough introspective self-examination, distinguishing carefully between those bits of our mental life that appear to arise endogenously (having "internal" causes), and those bits that appear to have been brought about by the activity of external causes. We set the former aside, and concentrate upon the latter. We attend to them as they present themselves in the very first moment of their entry upon the mental scene. The more we refrain from imposing any interpretation upon them, and the more passively we simply allow them to impress themselves upon us, the more cleanly and clearly we receive them new-minted from the hand of God and with the Form he gave them still clearly and distinctly impressed upon them.

Thus, provided that we can distinguish between the endogenously caused and the externally impressed bits of our subjective life, and provided that we really can apprehend and describe pure data just as they first present themselves to us and without any interpretation, then we really do have the beginnings of an autonomous body of purely man-made knowledge that, as it grows, can become independent of tradition and social authority. *Indeed, religious authority has been reluctantly obliged to certify the objectivity of this new body of knowledge that is going to emancipate us from it!* And the argument applies both to scientific knowledge and to religious knowledge. The Reformed believer who clearly recognizes his or her own merely human state of bondage and moral weakness, and then goes on to speak of her passive experience of the lively action of God's unmerited Grace in her own soul, has got *a bit of purely given religious experience*, and on that basis can claim a well-founded personal Assurance of salvation that is logically independent of the authority of the Visible Church; and similarly the natural scientist who carefully maintains a clear distinction between pure observation-reports, and the various humanly invented mathematical and other theoretical patterns into which they are fitted, has found a way to develop a new natural philosophy that is logically independent of authority and tradition.

The point being made here applies equally to Protestants, to mystics and to the new "experimental philosophers" (i.e., natural scientists). All of them want to break away from the old social and traditional control of knowledge. All want to claim that the individual alone can in principle attain genuine religious or empirical knowledge, just by assembling elements given within his or her own mental history. Since the presented data are bits of Creation, and already have a bit of intelligible Form printed on them, we can put them together exactly like pieces of a jigsaw puzzle, and so build up our own mental map of the objective world. We can be sure that it will be objectively True because authority certifies that there is a God, that he has finished and fully Formed the world, that he has made us both to know him and to fit into his world, and therefore that our minds are made by him in the image of his mind – and now we see how the great innovators in religion and natural philosophy were indeed craftily using themes from the tradition to emancipate themselves from tradition.[3] They used tradition against itself, and the new Cartesian and empiricist ideas of the mind as a blank slate, of pure uninterpreted experience, and of the ideal disengaged scientific observer – these ideas, that seem at first sight so innocent, were in fact very cunning and subversive.

As Descartes puts it: Original Sin may affect the human will. We may be too precipitate in judgement. But the world remains God's creation, and our perceptual and rational faculties remain predesigned by God accurately to mirror his world and to track the cosmic order. Thus even in terms of orthodox theology, the more passively we register our experience, and the less we risk corrupting it by interpreting it, the more accurately our mind must mirror the objective world-structure. So Descartes borrows from the old theological realism in order to justify his own scientific realism, and launches the Modern scientific enterprise with the confidence that will eventually enable it to overthrow dogmatic theology – and thereby get *itself* into difficulties again. For when it has finally overthrown theology, it will have overthrown itself too!

As we shall see shortly, the same paradox haunts the history of religious experience.

Religious Experience

One might say that "religious experience" – just that phrase – has a very short past, but behind it there is a very long history. From the earliest times, human beings seem to have valued altered states of consciousness, and to have associated them with religion. The basic techniques were discovered surprisingly early, and are still in use. Music, for example, is everywhere used in religious contexts because of its power to induce a light trance, to precipitate ecstatic states, and to sway communal feelings; and it now appears that even the Neanderthals may already have possessed a simple pentatonic musical instrument, a bone flute. Dancing, like drumming, can make one "high," and the wearing of an animal mask can help to take you out of yourself and into an animal identity. Both are attested in Paleolithic art.

Around the world people pursue intoxication by chewing plant materials, by infusing them in hot water, by fermenting them, and by smoking them. Such practices enter religion when, for example, Buddhists drink tea in meditation and Christians sip wine during worship; but they are also very old, for analysis of chemical residues in early pottery has recently taken the history of fermented liquor back almost to the beginnings of pottery itself.

The link between religion and this little cluster of long-known and much-treasured psychotropic techniques is very strong – so strong that it prompts one to consider a very curious hypothesis. Perhaps religion did not and could not exist among human beings until they had reached the point where they could make the distinction between "normal" and "altered" consciousness? That is to say, for there to be religion, three conditions must already have been fulfilled and in place:

1   Human beings must already have developed the sort of "normal" consciousness that comes with the ability to handle pronouns, personal names, etc.
2   They must have discovered and "socialized" various techniques for modifying consciousness, such as rhythmic music and dance, dressing up, ritual, and intoxicants.
3   They must have been *able to recognize as different*, and have had some special reason for valuing, sundry "altered" states of consciousness. The contrast between "normal" and "altered" consciousness, when recognized, becomes the basis for the contrast between the profane and sacred worlds.

In the present state of knowledge it is not possible to take this question much further, beyond observing that language (and therefore "normal" language-dependent subjective consciousness), and music (and therefore communal ritual, and "altered" states of consciousness), and therefore also religious ideology, may all have been around for some tens of thousands of years, and may even have belonged to other species of *Homo* besides our own. That there may have been more than one species of us, capable of language, art, morality, and religion, is an extraordinarily disturbing thought.

All this indicates that in a certain sense the history of mysticism and religious experience may well go back to the very beginnings of humanity. Yet in another and perhaps more important sense they are modern inventions.

The phrase "religious experience" was given its currency above all by William James, whose *The Varieties of Religious Experience*, subtitled *A study in human nature*, first appeared in June 1902. Hardly anybody before James had used the phrase or could have used it in precisely the sense he gave it. A medical man, a Darwinian, and the founder of scientific psychology in the Anglo-Saxon world, James does not understand "religious experience" in the old realistic or supernatural way, as the cognizing of something that is given to the soul from outside it and from "Above." James (for the most part) treats religious experience in an immanent way and as a function or capacity of human nature, much like "aesthetic experience" or "moral experience." By thus naturalizing religious experience, James hopes to make of it the starting-point for a new science of religion, and perhaps even one day for a new line of religious apologetics. The hope persisted until very recently in the publications of Alistair Hardy's Religious Experience Research Unit, established at Manchester College, Oxford.[4]

"Religious experience" then, in the sense of a particular way of understanding that specific English phrase, was born in about 1900 and died in about 1978, when the old liberal religious humanism was finally drowned by the rising tide of postmodern culturalism. After the publication of Stephen Katz' symposium (1978: see bibliography), people quickly acknowledged that religious experiences are everywhere couched in the locally available symbolic vocabulary. Every religious experience is a datable human cultural expression.

Before James, a number of nineteenth-century writers had indeed used the phrase, "religious experience." But their use of it is still realistic, and dependent therefore upon the older Protestant dogmatic theology. It also depends upon the stock phrase, "to experience religion." In George Eliot's *Scenes of Clerical Life* (1858), for example, we are told that "It may be that some of Mr Tryon's hearers had gained a religious vocabulary rather than religious experience." This is pure realism: the skill of using religious words correctly is one thing, and actually to experience in one's own soul the weight of sin and the overwhelming influx of God's unmerited Grace is quite another. It is curious that, although George Eliot had a good knowledge of German Idealist philosophy, she here still seems stuck in the old English contrast between "mere words," which are only secondary packaging, and "real things." But how could "real things" ever come to be and be recognized by us, except by the agency of words defining them and making them identifiable?

The earliest recorded English use of "religious experience" is another title: *A Diary of the Religious Experience of Mary Waring* (1809). Again, this is miles from William James. It is evangelical Protestant: Mary Waring is trying "to put into words" an account of the great things that God is doing day by day in her soul. These things seem to be too great for words, and they take place in the hidden realm of her soul. How can she publicize them? Answer: she can find adequate words only because God's Holy Spirit commands and empowers her to do it.

Here we come across a most important point. Following Augustine, Calvin summed up the whole of human knowledge and everything that is really important to us under two heads: the knowledge of God and the knowledge of ourselves.[5] The physical world of Nature and even the social world were by Calvin drastically secularized. So was reason, with the effect that there was no way to God either through the public world of empirical fact or by philosophy. The only way to God was through the impact of Scripture, God's self-revelation, within and upon the individual soul. The only true Church was not the public institution, but the Invisible Church of the elect, who are all those who have truly and inwardly "experienced religion."

Calvin's influence was very important in the creation of modern secular capitalist culture. But he taught, he *had* to teach, a supernaturalism of the soul, and he became a prime source of modern popular irrationalism through his doctrine of Assurance – the doctrine that you can acquire a sure and invincible confidence about matters of objective divine reality and about your own eternal salvation, purely on the basis of private and (supposedly) prelinguistic goings-on in your own psychology. This conviction of objectivity could be justified only if the old Catholic natural theology, and the old Catholic doctrine of the authority of the Church, were still securely in place. But they are *not*. Calvin is resting the whole weight of his argument upon his "supernaturalism of the soul." Everyone can now be their own Pope: each individual human subject has an interior hotline to the supernatural world. As for the common public world – it is secularized.

Thus there is a parallel between Calvin's theological realism and Descartes' scientific realism. Both men want to reach out, just through their own subjectivity, and hook on to something that they can know is objectively Real. To do this, each has to borrow a little bit of conviction-of-objectivity from the older tradition, and this unacknowledged borrowing makes each of them vulnerable.

Against this background one can see both why Calvinism and the Protestant type of appeal to religious experience once seemed so strong, and also why they have now collapsed so ignominiously. Since Darwin, modern scientific psychology has suddenly and violently secularized the soul, making psychology the most "unbelieving" of all academic disciplines.[6] In addition, great (though as yet little-understood) changes in philosophy have led us increasingly to put language before experience, Culture before Nature, and the public realm before the private. There are no prelinguistic yet cognitively privileged events in the soul. Everything in the soul is secondary, and there can be no question of having within it an access to the supernatural world that we cannot get through the public world.

Mysticism

In classical Greece one said *"Mu, mu,"* meaning "Sh! Sh!," keep *mum. Muein* meant to close the lips or eyes, and *musteria*, mysteries, were esoteric, occult, or secret religious practices such as the Eleusinian mysteries. A *mystic* then became a person initiated into a higher and secret form of knowledge. How was this higher knowledge gained? Various metaphors have been used: *ecstasy*, standing outside oneself, implies a jump into a higher, or at least a different, mode of consciousness; *illumination* implies a lighting-up of consciousness from Above; and *infused contemplation* implies the pouring-in of divine truth like a warm liquid. A large group of visual metaphors – intuition, vision, contemplation, *theoria* – are associated with a sharp contrast between two different ways of knowing. One may look at a shadow or reflection, or alternatively one may turn and look directly at the original. Ordinary knowledge is indirect or mediated; it is propositional or "discursive." It depends upon words and other symbols. But the mystic goes beyond all the images to seek an immediate knowledge of and union with the divine essence.

At this point doubt strikes: when knowledge has become fully immediate, can it still be called *knowledge*? In immediacy, there are no longer two; there is only one. So the language suddenly forks. The mystic's way of knowing God by union with God, being ineffable and non-discursive, goes so far beyond ordinary language-based knowledge that it cannot be compared with it. It should therefore be described as a state of darkness, emptiness and unknowing.

Alternatively, and following Plato's Allegory of the Sun, one may argue that, just as the Sun is the most highly visible object of all and the one that makes everything else visible, so the mystic's immediate visionary kind of knowing is the Prime Analogate, the standard sort of knowing, the paradigm case. We should put it first and see all the other levels of knowing as declensions from it.

Thus it is possible, from the same broadly Platonic and neoplatonic starting point, to argue *either* that the divine nature is utterly incomprehensible to us, and can be known by us only by unknowing and in a state of utter darkness; *or* that God is the most readily knowable and universally known object of all, the knowledge of him being the foundation or underpinning of all other knowledge whatsoever. The first line of argument leads to the conclusion that nobody can really know God, and the second to the conclusion that there can be nobody who does *not* know God. The two conclusions must coincide, the knowledge of God being something so deep and dark and transcendental that in one way nobody has it, and yet in another way everybody has it.

We can now indicate what is usually meant by "mysticism." In the monotheistic faiths at least, it is a tradition of devotional writing which commonly uses the vocabulary of Plato and the neoplatonists, and is rather consciously paradoxical. It discourses at length about the Ineffable, uses erotic metaphors to describe matters purely spiritual, and speaks in visual terms about the Invisible. In mystical experience, we learn, the subject–object distinction is transcended; yet such experience is always described as noetic. How can there be *knowledge*, where there is no longer any distinction between the knower and the known? And for that matter, how can the mystic or anyone else draw "nearer" to God, when theology says that God is already omnipresent in his whole being and power at every point in space and time? Everything and everyone, whether holy or sinful, is already as "close" to God as it is possible to be. God is always and everywhere already coincident with each and every human self. And, by the way, how is mystical experience able to be "simultaneously" "timeless" and "transient"?

Mystical writing is so steeped in such paradoxes – and there are many even more startling ones, yet to be explored – that some readers lose patience with it. But I shall later be suggesting that, as in the case of "metaphysical poetry," the paradoxes are there for a purpose, and one that needs to be better understood.

Meanwhile, it is sufficient to identify mysticism via a line of texts – devotional writings which use the language of Plato and neoplatonism, and which are consciously paradoxical. A mystical text often begins in very serious style. What follows is going to be dangerous stuff, we are told, and the frivolous reader is sternly warned off.[7] Then what follows? Play, paradox, highflown sentiment, linguistic contortions, and near-heresy. Union with God is described *exactly* as if it were female orgasm, by people who are not merely of the wrong sex, but not supposed to have any personal experience of such things anyway.

No very satisfactory explanation of all this has yet been given. Why not? Because the concept of mysticism and the construction of a canon of mystical writers is so recent. It is true that even as far back as the early eighteenth century we find that people such as William Law and John Wesley are quite well read in the writers we would now call mystical. But seventeenth- and eighteenth-century writers in general use the term "mysticism" only as a term of disparagement. In France, where the term originated, it was used by high-ranking churchmen to ridicule new-fangled, half-baked, and amateurish religious writing. A more favourable attitude, along with the first books *about* mysticism and the first attempts to draw up lists of canonical writers, dates from the 1830s to 1850s. Examples are J. Görres, *Die Christliche Mystik* (1836–42) and in Britain, *Hours with the Mystics* (1856) by a writer who died sadly young, R.A. Vaughan (1823–57).

Thereafter the classic and still-remembered books about "Christian Mysticism" were almost all written in the period 1890–1970. They quickly led to a public demand for the identification of a mystical tradition and a canon of writers in each of the other major religious traditions, and this was soon done for Jews, Muslims,[8] and Hindus, and at least attempted in the more difficult case of Buddhism.

So "mysticism," as a concept, a literary genre, and a canon of writers within each major religious tradition, and therefore as also a possibly universal essence of religion, is late-Modern. So *very* late-Modern as to be more-or-less datable to the period 1890–1970, which makes it coincide with the heroic age of psychology, the main period of activity of James, Freud, Jung, and their leading associates and followers. During that period there was a considerable elaboration of discourses about subjectivity, both by the introspective and literary psychologists and also by novelists and other imaginative writers. There were, it appeared, two sorts of space: there was the exterior geometrical space of the common physical world, and there was the "interior" but non-geometrical space of the psyche, a space very large and ancient but only ever partly lit. Below the illumin-ated surface of our conscious experience, rational thought, and accessible memories there lay a hinterland in which dark unconscious forces writhed and struggled for expression.

At this point it is important to recall that Arthur Schopenhauer had been the first modern philosopher to suggest that in the play of unconscious forces in the depths of the psyche we have each of us our own private access to the inmost nature of the world, "the Will."[9] Curiously, the first explicit atheist among the German philosophers thus appropriated for modernity a classic theme of "introvertive mysticism," the old doctrine that one could access noumenal reality just by introspection. Schopenhauer's influence helped to create a late-Modern culture preoccupied with subjectivity, a culture highly interested in *both* psychoanalysis *and* mysticism.

Spirituality

In terms of the classic binary oppositions around which our culture was formerly constructed, the word *spirituality* is the opposite of *temporality*. In Britain, well known to be the least-reformed country in the entire world, there remains to this day a body of "lords spiritual" who sit with the "lords temporal" in the Upper Chamber of Parliament; and "the spirituality" used to be simply the clergy, the body of ecclesiastical persons.

In Modern times, as human subjectivity became more and more highly valued, spirituality gradually came to mean piety. An expression such as "Benedictine spirituality" was used to signify the tradition of formal teaching about personal piety and the religious life that was to be found in a certain historical community.

Today, arguably, spirituality is already taking on a postmodern and expressionist sense, influenced no doubt by the way certain associated words such as culture and lifestyle are moving. Think, for example, about "gay culture," "gay lifestyle," and "gay spirituality." Perhaps your spirituality is now your own personal religious temper of mind, project, and lifestyle. As such, it seems to be purely human in its aims, and freely chosen. There is no longer any reference either to a voluntarily undertaken discipline, or to a series of stages of proficiency. Instead, in postmodernity spirituality has become aestheticized, and the religious life now increasingly takes the form of a demonstration, a performance or display. We make a show, not of the Blessed Sacrament in a monstrance, but of *ourselves*. Spirituality becomes "camp" – an interesting, irritating word which well brings out why many of today's strongest religious controversies are battles between the partisans of postmodern and Modern spiritualities. Thus, postmodern gay Christians may wish to use the Church as a theatre for the enactment of gay spirituality, a gorgeous symbolic display. They really very much want to do this, and one may well ask – Why not? Why ever not?

But of course theatrical, camp spirituality is intensely irritating to the old Modern outlook, which valued hiddenness. The old spirituality was a secret discipline of the inner life, defined within a tradition and freely embraced by the individual, who pursued it under the guidance of a spiritual director. Modern spirituality was usually *introvertive*; postmodern spirituality is usually *extravertive*,[10] a showiness that has the great merit of making it readily available to public inspection and debate. Modern spirituality liked to emphasize the contrast between outer appearance and inner reality; postmodern spirituality *comes out* all over the place. It makes a virtue of making an exhibition of oneself.

*   *   *   *

This discussion of the recent history of *experience, religious experience, mysticism,* and *spirituality* suggests that one day we may come to see modernity as having been a curious transitional stage in the history of thought.

Under the old Classical regime of Objective Rationalism, which remained solid at least until the fourteenth century, the world was ready-made for us by God. God was a language-user: God guaranteed the stability of language itself, and the fit between language and the world. All knowledge was received as gift. The "method of research" was to purify yourself in order to be illuminated from above.

In postmodernity, we ourselves, and also the many and varied worlds we build around ourselves, are all given within the flux of our language. There are no absolutes. Nothing is *purely* given: indeed, *contra* Descartes, there is no pure self to make a pure gift to. We, we, must make do and mend – in a flux that also makes and mends *us*.

Modernity was a transitional period during which heroic individuals constructed within human subjectivity a copy or representation of the ready-made world outside. It was a period of industrial espionage, in which enterprising Promethean humans stole God's plans in order to use them in building their own new version of the world. In a period of mind–body dualism the old belief in two worlds took a very curious new form. The world of the body was external Nature, the old objective Cosmos, and the world of the mind was the realm of the humanly imagined world-*picture*, the world represented in our knowledge, the world made of human symbols. The kind of Realism typical of modernity depended upon the idea of passive experience. The method of research was to collect within subjectivity clean data about the ready-made Cosmos out-there, and build within subjectivity a world-picture that neatly copied the reality out-there. Thus Modernity sought to combine themes from the old theology with the new emphasis on the human construction of our human knowledge. The man-made world inside would be an accurate replica of the old god-made world, which was still presumed to be *there*. In this context, some hoped that after its original theological guarantee had expired the world of subjective consciousness and man-made knowledge would be able to stand alone, completely autonomous and secular, while others hoped (as we shall see) that by the study of religious experience and mysticism it might be possible to establish a bridgehead of the supernatural within human subjectivity.

The paradigmatic human activity under Objective Rationalism was theoretical contemplation, either in philosophy or in religion; in modernity it was empirical science; and in postmodernity it is art, diffused by the new technologies.[11]

CHAPTER TWO

theories of
mysticism in
modernity

Modernity in Western culture arose out of medieval humanism, which from the beginning had a slight air of protest about it. It was the protest of human weakness against absolute power.

Thus in the Bull *Unam Sanctam* (1302) Urban VIII delivered what remains perhaps the grandest statement of the papal claims: "We declare, state, define and pronounce that it is altogether necessary to salvation for every human creature to be subject to the Roman pontiff." Objective rationalism and absolute monarchy have here become combined into a tight system. All questions of truth and value are already determined by an omnipotent Creator, and there is a clear chain of command: God, Christ, the Pope, the King, the Church, and the State authorities. There seems here to be no room at all for criticism or for any innovation. Absolute truth, absolute power, and absolute value coincide, in a way that leaves nothing for the individual human being except submissive acceptance of one's place in the all-powerful, all-knowing system.

Yet it is precisely in the fourteenth century, when a persecuting Church is still at the zenith of its power and religion has seemingly been reduced to political subjection, that we find the greatest flowering of mysticism and lay piety yet seen in Europe, and a notable shift away from theocentrism towards a more christocentric outlook, with the focus especially upon the Passion of Christ. This is the so-called *devotio moderna*, the very earliest form of modernity, seeking to bypass the command structure of the Church, undo the certainties of theology, enter the divine darkness, and share in the *human* suffering of Christ. Here we see Christian mysticism as a humanism, seeking to escape from and to undo absolutism.

For several centuries afterwards, the clearest common theme of emerging modernity was the desire to affirm the priority of, and to vindicate the point of view of, the finite individual human being. Could thoroughgoing anthropocentrism be made to work? Maybe it *could* be made to work, at least in the sorts of areas that had almost always been left to the poets and painters – human love, geometrical perspective, the vision of landscape, naturalism in art. Maybe it could also be made to work in areas of government, such as foreign policy and economics, that the Church had never really sought to take over. But altogether harder questions arose in areas such as theology, metaphysics, ethics, and the sciences of nature. In order to make any headway here against the old Objective Rationalism and its hugely powerful institutions, you had to claim that it was possible to get objectivity out of subjectivity: that is, you had to claim and to show that just from a starting-point within human subjectivity, and with only the ordinary human being's resources, you could build a system of objective knowledge that was better and more reliable than the old order. Somehow it had to be possible to argue from merely psychological premises, reporting human experiences, to metaphysical conclusions about how things really are out-there.

Much of the history of Western thought since the Middle Ages has revolved around the question: "Can it be done? Can human beings rebuild their world and all branches of knowledge around themselves, just on the basis of their own reason and experience, and get it right – or at least, right enough to be going on with?" In the natural sciences and in philosophy, many were confident that the answer was Yes. During the seventeenth century elements of the old system of thought were still being called upon to support the new, as when Descartes calls upon God to guarantee the veracity of our sense-experience and our innate conviction of the objective reality of the external world. But after Newton's achievement had been digested there was, understandably, great confidence in the power of unaided human reason to construct a complete fundamental science of nature; and if reason could do *that*, then surely it could do much else as well.

In religion and ethics, however, the story has turned out rather differently. Between Luther and Hegel it was widely thought that Protestantism was quite obviously intellectually stronger and more up-to-date than Catholicism; but today that is no longer so. Indeed, Protestantism today is (if anything) in poorer shape intellectually than is Catholicism. And if the cause of Protestantism is more-or-less identical with the cause of modernity, then the eclipse of the one must also mean the eclipse of the other. As for ethics, it is now widely agreed that the Enlightenment project, that of finding a new universal rational foundation for ethics, has failed; which again is a severe setback for the Modern cause.

So the position seems to be that the one huge success of the Modern and Enlightenment project has been experimental natural science. It may not quite give us demonstrable or "absolute" knowledge, but it has at least given us masses of working hypotheses good enough to be going on with. In other areas, the appeal to experience and to standard test procedures has simply not produced the same results. Despite all the hopes and all the attempts, we have not yet been able to build up either a science of religion on the basis of the appeal to religious experience, or a science of ethics on the basis of the appeal to common moral experience.

However, there is one consolation: we are fairly widely agreed on why we disagree so much. In natural science we have a standard world-wide vocabulary and standard checking-procedures; but in religion and morality, as also in art, we have many different and incommensurable traditions, each with its own distinctive vocabulary. These vocabularies mould the experience of the people who use them, to such a degree that it seems we never find any purely "natural" and uninterpreted data of moral, religious, or aesthetic experience. So we don't have standard universal concepts, and we don't have standard universal pure experiences. It is this absence of pure and prelinguistic experiences to test theories by that has prevented the development of sciences of ethics, art, and theology.

However, in the mid-nineteenth century, as knowledge of the great Asian and other non-Western traditions develops, the claim begins to be made by some that the long-sought cross-cultural religious universals have at last been found. The Enlightenment search for a universal "natural religion" certainly did fail, but mysticism looked much more promising precisely because in several traditions the introvertive mystics made such a deliberate effort to abstract away from local symbolism and the local vocabulary. So perhaps the higher levels of mystical experience may provide the clean, uncontaminated experimental data that a new science of religion calls for? What we need is pure psychological data, prior to any structuring by theory or coding into language; and perhaps introvertive mysticism was a systematic attempt to create a state of mind in which precisely such data could be acquired?

All this background then helps to explain why there was so much interest in mysticism during the later Modern period, and why the theoretical arguments about mysticism took the form they did.

In the first place, and in accordance with the usual course of Modern thinking, mystical texts were understood to contain descriptions of mystical states, which in turn were thought of as being, needing to be, pure non-linguistic states of consciousness. It was very often said that such uninterpreted states were "ineffable," because in them one was absorbed, passive, and plunged into an undifferentiated unity. It is not just that there is no difference within the field of consciousness, but also that the conscious self is itself not differentiated from the field. It is "lost" in timelessness and speechlessness, enraptured.

To us postmoderns it is very obvious that writing of this sort is reflexively paradoxical. How can one describe a state as being indescribable? How can I pretend to remember that *at some past moment* I was so rapt that I was out of time altogether? Indeed, how can someone pretend to remember and to describe a state of being so lost in immanence that he can be in no condition to remember anything?

However, Modern thinking was (and, of course, still remains) as a rule strangely unaware of language and unaware of reflexivity problems, and it disregarded these considerations. It greatly needed mystical experiences to be in at least some ways comparable with pure sense-experiences, so that they could offer experimental confirmation of religious beliefs, rather as sense-experiences may confirm scientific hypotheses. Mystical experiences therefore had to be passively received or "infused," and also prelinguistic, in order to be clean: and in addition they needed to be available cross-culturally, if religious beliefs were ever to achieve the sort of anywhere-in-the-world checkability that we have come to expect in the case of natural science.

So *in the second place* it was also claimed that mystical experiences are noetic. In them, one feels one knows something: indeed, one feels one knows it all. This is certainly very odd; for how can there be *knowledge* that is prior to language and that is even prior to any distinction of subject and object? The best reply one can give on behalf of the Moderns is that the very paradoxicality of mystical states is a sign that they involve not just ordinary empirical knowledge, but knowledge of a Transcendent Object. Here the idea is doubtless that, if a human psychological state is to be a cognition of something beyond the world of experience, then it surely has to be paradoxical. But how do we *know* that mystical states are would-be cognitions of transcendent reality? One suspects that in the period before Buddhist meditation was well understood, writers about mysticism tended simply to assume that mystical states were everywhere states of consciousness reached by persons who were seeking to *know* something very great, and something ordinarily unknowable, namely God. And indeed, around the world people have tended to equate feeling a bit drunk with being "enthused" – i.e., "in God." A manic state is assumed to be a supernatural cognitive state.

During the Modern period – at least, between the early seventeenth and the early twentieth centuries – philosophy was in every field trying to overcome scepticism and to vindicate realism. Starting within the individual human subject, one hoped to move from sense-experiences to knowledge of "the external world," from moral experience to knowledge of an objective moral order, from the most general features of the world of experience to the existence of God, and so on. Any and every sort of "experience" was considered to be "veridical" insofar, and only insofar, as it lent support to realism. Your experience was genuine, authentic, veridical if and only if through it you had knowledge of something independently real and existing out-there. Knowledge of objective reality was the Supreme Good, that preceded everything else and was more important than anything else.

Now, today, you are a postmodern if you see how strange, how gratuitous, was the old Modern preoccupation with realism. *Why?* Why the frantic obsession with knowledge and, in particular, with objectivity? The answer, surely, is that from its beginnings modernity was on the defensive. The ecclesiastical defenders of established authority and Objective Rationalism ridiculed it. They said it was sure to get bogged down in scepticism, subjectivism, and even solipsism. If you start within individual subjectivity you will never fully escape it. You will always be haunted by doubts about "other minds," about "the external world," about "the moral law." Tradition's attack upon early modernity was so formidable that it is scarcely surprising that something of an arms-race mentality developed. Vindicating realism became an obsession, to such an extent that almost every scrap of our subjective life came under scrutiny in the hope that it might be used to "prove the objectivity" of something or other.

Contrary to what might be thought, modernity remained for centuries keen to establish its own religious respectability. Theological realism was dominant, but a Modern religious writer could not argue for the existence of God either simply from authority, or from the traditional metaphysical premises. What was most needed was a proof of the existence of God from purely psychological premises; and during the nineteenth century a whole range of new-style theistic proofs was accordingly developed. These were arguments for the existence of God from "the feeling of absolute dependence" (Schleiermacher), from aesthetic feeling (Victor Cousin), from moral experience (Newman, the neo-Kantian theologians, and others), from the felt consciousness of one's own moral freedom (ibid.) and indeed from the uniqueness and irreducibility of subjective consciousness as such.

Pressing further, early twentieth-century writers go on to argue that in one's experience of a fellow-human being there is something immeasurable, ultimate, and so implicitly theological (Martin Buber, and perhaps Emmanuel Levinas). Others have argued that feelings can be and often are cognitive (e.g., Cook Wilson).[1] One may have an entirely veridical feeling-that, it is claimed; and so "arguments from religious experience" have been developed. If a mere feeling can be propositional, then it can enter into an argument.

This background explains why the late-Modern interest in mysticism and religious experience took the form that it did. It was above all an *apologetic* interest. People very much wanted to demonstrate that religious experience and mysticism were or could be "veridical," which meant that they could provide experimental or experiential verification of the existence of God, which in turn meant that philosophical realism would be vindicated. In the biggest way possible, we'd have got out of our own subjectivity to make contact with the really Real – which is that we most of all want to do.

Determinedly, tenaciously, late-Modern writers (who are still around in large numbers) have clung to their own identification of the cause of religion with the cause of philosophical realism. When mysticism and religious experience are looked at from their point of view, three theories are possible: realism, semi-realism, and naturalism.

Realism

A well-known (and rather early-Modern) exponent of a realistic interpretation of religious experience is the Oxford philosopher of religion Richard Swinburne.[2] He begins from what he calls "the Principle of Credulity" – the presumption of commonsense and of the law courts that the testimony of honest and sincere witnesses is to be taken at face value, unless and until we find reasons for doubting it. Now, great numbers of ordinary folk declare that they have personally experienced the presence of God, the Grace of God, and also the Will of God, pressing upon them in their sense of being subject to moral obligation. Considerable numbers of people have also reported visions of, for example, Christ or the Virgin Mary. Others, we might add, have been vividly conscious of the presence of their dead mentors and relatives. In all these cases there is no doubt that ordinary people's conviction of objectivity is very strong. They claim that their moral experience leaves them in no doubt of its own objectivity, and similarly that their religious experience also strikes them as being a datum, a gift. It is not an objectless feeling; it is a feeling-*that* they are in the presence of a higher Power.

But if there is indeed a God, a wise ethical Creator who desires us to live according to his will and in fellowship with him, then surely these reported facts of moral and religious experience are just what we might have expected? And therefore if we have some independent reason for holding that it is more likely than not there is indeed such a God, then we have that much reason for accepting also that ordinary people's moral and religious experience, with its claim to objectivity, is veridical. More: we can adduce it as corroborative evidence.

There is also a further point. When people experience God, they speak of warmth and light, even though God, not being material, cannot "literally" be thought of as radiating either heat or light. And they often speak of God as communicating with them in human language, even though God cannot be thought of as being "literally" a member of a human language-group. In addition, when they see Mary, they are likely to see her in the full panoply of Catholic iconography: she wears a red gown and a blue cloak, her face shines, and the moon and stars are beneath her feet.

Swinburne thinks that all this can be interpreted realistically through the traditional doctrine of accommodation, according to which God in communicating with us accommodates himself to our capacities. If Mary is to be recognized by me *as* Mary, she must appear looking like her image in the local church, and she must appear in the skin colour, whether black, yellow, or white, which is most familiar to me. If she speaks, she must speak the local dialect, or I will not understand her. And similarly, God must appear in the guise of a very great and awesome human father or king: he must assume his own familiar imagery in order to make himself known to human beings.

Semi-realism

Since the old theological realism builds the world around God and makes God the cause of everything, it naturally looks to God, and not to human history or psychology, for an explanation of the regional variations of religious experience. Mary's various personal appearances on Earth, for example, must be carefully preplanned from the heavenly end. She must be kitted out for each occasion with the right skin-colour, costume, dialect, message to deliver, and so on; and there must be no mistakes. Think how traumatic it would be if she were to speak the wrong dialect, or to garble her message! Fortunately, one has never heard of a theophany, or of any other 'ophany of a denizen of a supernatural world, in which the one who appeared wore the wrong clothes or fluffed her lines. It just doesn't happen, does it?

If the old belief that in Revelation the divine realm "accommodates" itself to local human expectations and vocabularies now seems rather comical, that is because our religious thinking has become so anthropocentric. Under the influence of German Idealist philosophy since Kant and Hegel, and French social theory since Durkheim, we have come to take it for granted that belief shapes perception, and that people's religious experience is always couched in the local vocabulary available to them. Everywhere, religion is "culturally patterned interaction with culturally postulated supernatural beings"; everywhere religion is human and historically evolved; everywhere religion borrows vocabulary from the human realm. The old realism claimed that it was the gods who took the initiative and did everything first: they gave us fire, they taught us metalworking, and so on. But from the point of view of the new humanism, our language, our social relations, and our technology must have come first: it was only *after* we had invented metalworking that it became possible for us to believe in a god of metalworking. Only *after* human beings have begun to think of building spaceships does human religious experience begin to include apparitions of flying saucers.

So technological change brings it about that in the USA people who in the past would have been possessed by evil spirits are nowadays abducted by aliens. Religious experience is bound to be clad in the most imaginatively potent vocabulary currently available.

Very well: religious thought and experience are everywhere human and cultural, couched in the local vocabulary. Does it follow that religion everywhere is a sort of communal science fiction, an imaginative projection of current human desires, fears, and dreams?

Not necessarily, says semi-realism. The huge growth of our knowledge of other cultures and religions since the late eighteenth century has drawn attention not only to the human diversity of religion, but also to some possible cross-cultural universals: for example, the parallels noted by many since Schopenhauer between the histories of Indian and Western philosophy, the similarity of introvertive (or unitive) mysticism in many traditions, the almost universal aspiration after a transcendent reality or a supernatural world, the sense of the Holy, or the "numinous," and finally certain very widespread "archetypal" patterns of myth and symbolism. All these factors surely suggest that in religion everywhere there is a common core.

Against this background, semi-realism typically claims that there is in all religious thought and experience a veridical core-intuition, clad in very variable human cultural imagery. Behind the outward or "phenomenal" diversity of religion there is one ultimate noumenal Reality.

John Hick's large book *An Interpretation of Religion* (1989) is entirely concerned with attempting to make, explain, and defend a claim of this type. He makes a distinction between "the Real as it is in itself" and the Real "as it is thought and experienced through our human religious concepts."[3] However, his lengthy discussion leads him to acknowledge that not even the way of unitive mysticism arrives at an agreed universal account of the Real that transcends all local differences of vocabulary. Even among the unitive mystics, It is for some quasi-personal, for others impersonal; for some Emptiness, and for others the fullness of Being; and for some wholly Other, whereas for others It is radically immanent in the flux of experience. "All that we can say," says Hick, "is that we postulate the Real *an sich* as the ultimate ground of the intentional objects of the different forms of religious thought-and-experience."[4] So "the Real" is not real after all. It is out of sight. It is a point of convergence so remote that not even the unitive mystic actually reaches it. Hick has given no reason, and has admitted that he *can* give no reason, for describing it as the "Real," rather than as merely an ideal focus of aspiration. All he can say is that in using religious language *he intends* it to have real reference, and he thinks that most ordinary people have always intended realism. Furthermore, he describes open non-realism as being élitist and unkind to all those humble folk who need to believe in a posthumous compensation for the wretchedness of this life.[5] So we feel we ought to be realists; and one might say that Hick's theological realism consists only in nostalgia for realism and reluctance to part with it.

Here, Hick's situation is similar to Locke's over the doctrine of substance, and to Kant's over the thing-in-itself. Locke says quite enough to destroy the idea of substance. It is not given to us either by sensation or reflection. It is unexperienceable. It is an imaginary point of anchorage, "the supposed but unknown support of those qualities we find existing, which we imagine cannot subsist *sine re substante*, without something to support them."[6] In fact, the old idea of substance is very clearly shown by Locke to be a "theological" idea, in the bad sense. Without any grounds, we have a deep persistent hunch that the secondary, the transient, is unsatisfactory and can't exist by itself: there has to be a unifying, sustaining higher-order Reality that props it all up and holds it together. How, we don't know; all we know is that we have that hunch.

Locke sees all this, yet somehow he can't give up the old realism, just as Kant could see perfectly well that the idea of the thing-in-itself does no useful work at all, but somehow couldn't quite bring himself openly to discard it. Berkeley and Hegel had no such inhibitions; and in the same way Hick's minimal and nostalgic version of theological realism is bound to be discarded by his successors.

There are two further – and, as I think, fatal – difficulties in Hick's position. The first is philosophical: the distinction between God *a se* and God *quoad nos* (God-in-himself, and God-as-he-appears-to-be-to-us) may be makeable within the thought-world of medieval philosophy and theology, but it cannot be made in modern critical philosophy. We are always inside our own heads and inside our own language; we see everything only from our own human angle, and we cannot pretend to be able to lay aside our own human limitations and contemplate God – or indeed any other supposed object of knowledge – in an absolute and perspectiveless way.

Second, if there is one thing about what we learn from our meditation and contemplative prayer upon which human beings are generally agreed, it is that we find ourselves led by it into an experience of non-dual, undifferentiated unity. It is a desert of vast eternity. This non-dual mystical experience may be interpreted, perhaps, in terms of either monism or nihilism: but how can it possibly be thought to confirm, or even be compatible with, metaphysical *dualism*? As we shall see in due course, the practice of mystical prayer is, and is intended to be, a *cure* for realistic theism, and not a confirmation of it.

Naturalism 1

As we have remarked already, during the late-Modern period writers *about* mysticism and religious experience (as distinct from the authors of mystical texts themselves) have been preoccupied with the question of realism. Can there be a valid argument from psychological premises to dogmatic metaphysical conclusions? Can any religious experiences be read as experimentally verifying religious beliefs, and can there be in mystical experience a direct intuition of God?

Traditional Realism answered in the affirmative. If there really is a God, then surely God may be expected to grant veridical experiences of his Presence to those who most ardently seek him? And Realism adds that the more obviously human and culturally specific features of religious experiences may be seen as "accommodations," in which God adapts his self-disclosure to the faculties of the people to whom he is revealing himself.

Semi-realism, a more recent view, goes further. It fully admits, as we have seen, the human and culturally conditioned character of all religious language, practice and experience. But, it says, if there is in human beings something that transcends this life and looks beyond it to a supernatural destiny, then we may and should claim to *intend objective reference* for our prayers and our aspirations after God. But semi-realism of John Hick's type cannot either prove the existence of God, or explain at all how the purported objective reference of religious utterances and aspirations is actually achieved. Like Descartes and Calvin, as we saw, it nostalgically claims more objectivity than it is entitled to.

Beginning with Spinoza, Modern religious naturalism renounces the claim that in mystical and religious experience we somehow pass beyond this present world. Religious expression does indeed refer, and it emancipates. One might say that its symbolic language "enlarges" life; but it acts within and is about this world and this life only, and this bringing-down of everything into just the one world-and-life continuum has the effect of returning religious metaphors into the everyday social, emotional, and sexual contexts from which they were drawn.

Against this background, what I am calling *Naturalism 1* emerges in the last quarter of the eighteenth century with the Kantian doctrine of the Sublime, the discovery of landscape, the rediscovery of Spinoza by Goethe and the Romantics, and the work of the early Schleiermacher, Caspar David Friedrich and many others.[7] Religious feeling is transferred from the old transcendent God to the world, the Whole of which we are part. In death, Shelley says of Keats, "He is made one with Nature" – not God any longer, but simply Nature; and to a surprising degree communion with Nature replaces communion with God. The mystical consciousness is a way of feeling utterly happy in one's own radical immanence in the world: one resonates *In Tune with the Infinite* (to quote the title of a hugely popular Victorian book).

In Spinoza, the great pioneer of the philosophy of Immanence, these ideas are presented in rationalist form. The mystic's experience of unity, "the intellectual love of God," is a completely clear, joyful, sane, and free consciousness of the oneness of subjective with Objective Reason. This is a mysticism of light, and of self- and world-affirmation. Everything is clearly understood to be what it must be, and one has no cause for discontent of any kind: nothing is obscure, and there is nothing from which one is alienated.

Naturalism 2

A second type of naturalistic interpretation of the religious consciousness is referred to by William James as a form of "medical materialism," and as "the sex theory."[8] It floats in the air of the times, he says in 1902; and James deals rather perfunctorily with it. J.H. Leuba (1925)[9] essays a fuller treatment, but even he does not make the point that needs to be made here, which is that the language in which mysticism and religious experience are written about is to a very great degree not just erotic, but female-erotic: that is, steeped in watery imagery expressing both our feelings for Woman, and the sexual pleasure of Woman. To anticipate a conclusion to be reached much later, it is as if the entire literature of mysticism and religious experience incorporates a feminine protest against, and a corrective for, the dour alienated masculinism of official doctrine and of social authority.

We begin by noting that in its rapture the soul is dissolved, melted, flooded, drowned:

> . . . Till in the ocean of thy love
> We lose ourselves in Heav'n above.
>
> . . . Dissolve my soul in ecstasies
> And bring all Heav'n before my eyes

The Christian believer descends into the waters of the womb, of Christ's death, of the font, and there drowns and is reborn. New life wells up, flows like a river. God pours out his Spirit. Grace erupts into the soul like a jet of warm liquid. It tastes sweet.

Imagery like this is most abundantly present in Latin Christianity, and in the poetry of the medieval *Vīraśaivas* or *Lingayatas* of India. That the old Hindu saints turned female sexuality very directly into mystical religion is well known. But what about such difficult and domineering male celibate priests as St Jerome and St Bernard of Clairvaux: how do they *know*, and what are they up to? In his extant letters to his female penitents, sundry Roman society ladies, Jerome tells them *exactly* what they will feel when the Bridegroom comes to them in the night. Christ will slip in, he tells the young Julia Eustochium,

> ... and will touch your belly; and you will start up all trembling, and will cry: "I am wounded with love."[10]
> (*et tangent ventrem tuum, et tremefacta consurges et dices Vulnerata caritatis ego sum*: Letter 22)

And so on, and on. We are told that St Bernard similarly, in his sermons on the Song of Songs (3, §§2–3),

> ... distinguishes between the successive stages of kissing Christ's feet, his hands and his mouth; and the kiss of the feet, with which we begin, is like the kiss of the sinful woman in the Gospel, the kiss of fear and penitence, as we wait prostrate for the Lord's words of forgiveness.

"Bernard," Rowan Williams continues, "compares the union of self and God with the mixing of water in wine ...". Warming to his theme, he speaks of how we should learn "ever greater openness to the pressure of God's love."[11] If that is not explicit enough, he continues while expounding Eckhart: "having arrived at that nakedness where the naked reality of God can enter, the soul is fertilized into divine life."[12] Hm.

It is not necessary here to dwell at length upon the familiar eroticism of wounds, of thraldom, bondage, and ravishment, for everyone knows that both in India and in the West spiritual writing makes extensive use of erotic imagery. What has not hitherto been sufficiently noticed or explained is the extent to which celibate male, as well as celibate female, writers unhesitatingly adopt the point of view and the metaphoric of specifically female sexuality for devotional writings.

*   *   *   *

Modern theories of mysticism, as put forward for the most part in the period around 1890–1970 (and, I must admit, still being written), were in all sorts of ways deeply unsatisfactory. Their over-riding interest in either finding empirical support for, or finding a replacement for, realistic theism is, to say the least, a distraction. It led them into the serious mistake of trying to find, isolate, write about, and make theoretical use of supposedly pure, culture-neutral and prelinguistic psychological states. This was a wild-goose chase. We can't use writing to reach such states, and even if they *could* be reached in some way, they couldn't possibly do anything to justify any form of Realism. Today mysticism has a bad name. Let's see if we can rehabilitate it.

dogmatic theology is an ideology of absolute spiritual power

Our great historic religious belief-systems are now slipping away from us very rapidly. Many or most people will have known a moment when they have paused in wonderment, suddenly aware that they can simply no longer *understand* a belief, a form of words, that once seemed to them both perfectly clear and very precious. What's happening to us?

Soon, we are going to feel the need for better explanations of religious belief-systems: how they were put together, what function they served, and what machinery was at work to make them seem meaningful in one age but then almost incomprehensible only a generation or so later.

So far, theology, as a subject, a kind of writing, has concerned itself largely with expounding, defending, modifying, and perhaps in various ways reinterpreting religious belief-systems. There has been an immense amount of research into the historical origins and development of religious beliefs, and various mythical and psychological theories of meaning have been put forward – suggesting, for instance, that we may compare religious belief-systems with dreams, and interpret them along similar lines. But there has not as yet been much in the way of clear explanations of why, for example, the great Christian dogmas of the Trinity and the Incarnation had to take just the form they did, and not some other form. And what influences operated to make it all seem to make sense for so long?

One of the first modern writers to begin to ask the right questions here was Walter Bauer, whose *Orthodoxy and Heresy in Earliest Christianity* first appeared in German in 1934.[1] Bauer began the deconstruction of the very words "orthodoxy" and "heresy." Both of these terms are "floating" and political. Neither of them has any stable referent. What they are at any one time taken to refer to depends on where you stand, and on the current state of play in various power-games. There never was just one original, orthodox, and apostolic Faith, sailing through history like a great ship guided by Providence, always successfully detecting and repelling heretics, and gradually building itself up and defining itself more clearly. That old story is a self-justifying myth, history as written by the victors. "What actually happened" was something very different. The earliest forms of Christianity accessible to us already include an extraordinary variety of beliefs and points of view, a variety that is still reflected in the canonical New Testament books, taken together with the now very large body of surviving extra-canonical writings[2] and other early sources. These many schools of thought struggled against each other, each trying to seize the high ground, each claiming to be the authentic and original faith. In this long battle for legitimacy a great number of criteria of truth were appealed to: a lineage of oral tradition, what was standard teaching at one of the major teaching-centres, the teaching of some great authority, scriptural exegesis (helped out by a good deal of quiet but systematic corruption of the scriptural texts),[3] baptismal formulae, authoritative rulings (where such were available and were recognized), personal revelations, and so on. Late antiquity was almost like the postmodern world: everybody, but *everybody*, seemed to behave like a member of a confused but very combative minority-group.

Finally, in the fourth century the priestly ruling group, or "hierarchy," the bishops, were prompted by the Emperor to meet in ecumenical councils and to start producing authoritative statements. What they gradually evolved, agreed, and enforced came to be regarded as "orthodoxy," just because and only because it was their teaching, the point of view that had prevailed *de facto* and in due course had become lawful, and so right *de jure*.

The orthodoxy that evolved in the fourth century came to seem meaningful for two reasons: it had become the official, legally approved, and dominant teaching, and furthermore, having been formulated by the bishops it was in their language and served their interests. *Cui bono?* Religious truth in the West is very highly political: one understands an idea when one understands who gains from it, and how. When I understand what's in it for me, I say: "Now you're talking sense!" In some such way as that, orthodoxy just was episcopal ideology, and "made sense" as such.[4] Charismatic religious leadership of the sort offered by Gnostics, Montanists, and such like was set aside. The Church, now an established catholic institution, needed and possessed the institutional leadership of a brotherhood of high priests. Priests are mediators between God and humans: Christianity itself is now seen as a faith in which salvation is institutionally mediated through a ministry and a sacramental system that are derived by an orderly process of historical trans-mission from Christ himself, the one true Mediator and our great High Priest.

Everything that is rightly said about Christ is shaped by the ideological need to demonstrate the cosmic finality and plenit-ude of the salvation that he has won for humankind, and that is mediated to us by the priests and the sacraments of the Church. Christ firmly bridges the God–Man divide. He is not a phantom or a vision but a fully human being, body and soul like us. Yet he is also God's only and eternally begotten Son, coequally divine, of one substance with the Father. He is not subordinate, he is not a co-opted Son, and his Christhood was not a super-added principle that abandoned him as he died.[5] In him the plenitude of divinity is personally, and henceforth inseparably, united to the plenitude of humanity. Quite straightforwardly, he is himself final salvation, fully achieved in his own Person. In him the whole gap is fully bridged, equally solidly on both sides of the God–Man divide.

What is said about the all-round plenitude of Christ's Incarna-tion and his saving work is thus designed to give maximum ideological support to the clergy and to the channels of grace that they control. But may not the argument be pressed somewhat further? If Christ, just by being "God from everlasting, Man for evermore," has already finished and perfected his atoning work, surely we are all saved already? In his divinity he is omnipresent, and in his human nature he is (technically) universal. He has become not just *a* man, but Man in general. His human nature, being universal, already includes both yours and mine. In which case surely every human being is already united with God in the same way that Christ is, and God is already everything in everyone? And if Christ's redeeming work is done, and the Creation is already reconciled with its Creator, then clearly there is no longer any need for the Church as a distinct social institution, nor for priests and sacraments, nor even for any theology that objectifies God as the Creator, a being ontologically distinct from his Creation. If redemption is complete then everything is already one continuous, universally reconciled, blissful totality. Is that not so?

We don't need to be told: we know perfectly well that we went astray in the last paragraph by drawing the wrong inference. Somehow we just know that although Christianity purports to be a religion of redemption, and although one is to believe that the final Victory has in a certain sense already been won, somehow no religion can ever actually complete its delivery of salvation within the historical order. As an historically persisting institution mediating salvation, the Church, the clergy and the sacramental system are perennially at work handing out pledges and tokens of a salvation that is never quite fully actualized. It cannot quite come: it *must* not come. While history endures, the divine and the human must remain radically distinct. Final salvation is always ahead, always just out of reach, awaiting us after death or at the end of time.

As I said, somehow everybody knows that from the agreed premise that Christ's redeeming work is done, finished, and complete we are *not* meant to conclude that final beatitude is immediately accessible to everyone here and now. It is such unwritten rules as these, prescribing what doctrinal inferences may and may not be drawn,[6] that are the real key to the meaning of every system of doctrine. We know beyond a doubt that we must not claim that the mystics' Unitive State is accessible by each individual here and now, because the Church's entire doctrine-system was developed and made orthodox by the hierarchy. They *own* it. Their own spiritual power, their standing, is derived from the belief-system and the great sacramental machine that they built up and they control; so *of course* the belief-system must not be interpreted in a way that could make them redundant. We know that. The doctrine-system must be read as confirming them in their present position, not as throwing them out of work.

So the Church perpetually teaches the achieved union of divinity and humanity in Christ, and perpetually must fail to deliver what it promises. The promise that the two worlds are now united is maintained by an institution that must insist on keeping them distinct. Christ is caught here in an awkward double-bind that must embarrass him greatly. On the one hand, he is himself the achieved actuality of final salvation in his own person, but on the other hand, his cosmic authority is called upon to guarantee the whole mighty apparatus – the sacred power and authority of the Church, the Bishops and the sacramental channels of Grace – that keeps final salvation deferred and out of our reach. Christ's authority as Saviour is used to prop up the very system that keeps salvation perpetually *deferred*! He is the *pons*, the Bridge to God: the Bridge is already there, built and finished, but we cannot and we must not claim to have completed the crossing. In this life, we will always need the Bridge-builder (Latin: pontifex, pontiff) to be guiding us across the Bridge. But it's a rubber Bridge, that gets longer and longer as we walk over it. We are always on the way: we will never reach the other side.

I am not complaining about all this. If an institution is to survive in history, and to retain a recognizable identity, then the old men must move in and draw up a constitution and a form of government. There will need to be established recognizable codes, structures, due processes, degrees of male rank and spiritual power, honours, traditions, and all the rest. The old boys fix all this up with alacrity, and having established it all, they want it to last. But in what purports to be a religion of salvation all these things seem to be incongruous, and as they become established one would expect also to see an emergent tradition of protest, a counter-culture.

It is clear what form the counter-cultural protest will take. It will attempt to deconstruct or undermine the various boundaries and lines of distinction by means of which the Church battles to postpone salvation and keep itself in business. It will try to achieve here and now the religious happiness that the orthodox machine promises, but will never deliver.

* * * *

From this discussion a prior and more difficult question now arises. How did the supposed need for salvation arise in the first place? What led people first to postulate a God or gods infinitely different from themselves, from whom they were radically alienated, yet with whom they must at all costs be reconciled? Why the initial presumption that the religious consciousness must be an unhappy consciousness, caught in an impossible contradiction? How can I even *know* that I yearn for and am in desperate need of Something that is infinitely different from me, unknowable, and inaccessible to me?

Theologians have often said that the old conciliar definitions of the Christian doctrine about Christ must fail because they cannot avoid self-contradiction. The divine and human natures and realms had been defined as opposites, in such a way that sentences about Christ describing how he bridges the gap and unites the two in his own person must assert impossibilities and contain contradictions. Very well – but in that case, surely, further analysis will trace the contradictions back into the supposed human condition that Christ has come to remedy? In which case we find in the doctrine of redemption an impossible solution that is impossible precisely because it has been so carefully tailored to fit an impossible problem.

Why then the impossible problem? After all, human life has not *always* been lived in a state of alienation from the supernatural world. On the contrary, it appears that in Paleolithic and early-Neolithic religion there was no rigid barrier between human consciousness and the world of the gods. People very readily fell into entranced or ecstatic states in which – so it seemed to them – humans, animals, spirits, and gods mingled. One could easily identify with, or mate with, or be transformed into a being of a quite different kind. Shamans journeyed through the supernatural world and gods walked with humans. But the myths relate that there came a time (it was the beginning of history) when the gods withdrew to the supernatural world and ceased to appear in person among humans. The old easy promiscuity was forbidden. There were to be no more centaurs, mermaids, or demigods. The Cosmos was now seen as having been divided up into clearly defined zones. The Law ordained that everything was to stay in its own place and to mix only with its own kind. The Cosmos became sharply class-stratified, and gods and humans in particular came increasingly to be described in binary opposition to each other. God is spirit, you are flesh; God is in Heaven, you are on Earth; God is all-powerful, you are weak; God knows everything, you know nothing; God is immortal, you are a mere mortal; God is holy, you are a sinner; God is always the Judge, you are always the guilty defendant who must cast yourself upon his mercy.

To understand the logic here, it is necessary to recall that until late-Modern times the leading attributes of God were his omnipotence and his unconditional judicial authority. God was God Almighty, a fearsome but utterly inescapable Judge and King, to whom one was subject.

People sometimes ask for "evidence of the existence of God"; but we should ask ourselves: where in the world of human experience do we still find a principle of unconditionally sovereign power and authority? The answer is straightforward: such a principle is the *arche* or foundation of the sovereign nation-state, and something similar appears also in a few other closely allied institutions, military and religious.

The idea of pure unlimited sovereign power and authority, the core idea around which and upon which the State is built, is bodied-forth or symbolized in a variety of different ways. It may be embodied in an image of a god, or in a divine king, or in a priest-king, or even in a modern form of words such as "the Queen in Parliament," or "the sovereign people." It may be vested in the insignia of sovereignty, such as a throne, a crown, an orb, and a sceptre. Quite often it is embodied in a rock: there are rocks that act as foci at Mecca (the Ka'ba), at Jerusalem (the Temple Mount and the Dome of the Rock), at Rome (where *Petros, Peter* is himself a sort of human rock), and in for example Scotland, which has a Stone of Destiny. Some English villages still have Anglo-Saxon Stones of Judgement.

The central, founding, ruling principle of power and judicial authority in the State was from the first and still is a highly theological idea. A domain is unified under an invisible transcendent sovereign immortal principle, which acts to divide the human race into two categories: fellow-citizens and foreigners, believers and infidels, we and they, the house of peace and the house of war. To this day we take it almost entirely for granted that, because we live in a State society and cannot choose not to, the world is divided into those people for whom we may be ordered to lay down our lives, and those people whom we may be ordered to kill. And yes – the State and its demand upon us does have just the terrifying inescapability that we have traditionally associated with God. Like God, it demands an unconditional allegiance even unto death, it rewards and punishes, it remembers for ever.

The suggestion is, then, that the old easy commerce between the human world and the supernatural world was brought to an end by the rise of the first law-governed State societies. The gods withdrew to Heaven and became fearsome and remote. Henceforth they communicated with humans only via the Law and the great officers of the State. To make the State work, our relations with the gods had to become institutionalized or bureaucratized. We had to lose the old face-to-face intimacy. Thus religious alienation became the "normal" condition of the human being in a State society. In this life there is nothing better for us than obedience to religious law, and the hope perhaps of a more direct experience of the divine after death.

Over much of the world, the sovereign nation-state is now almost the only truly "theological" thing we have left. Our religious institutions are too weak to be theological in the strong sense any longer. Only in Islam does something like a fully theological religious set-up survive, still retaining much of its ancient overwhelming and terrifying coercive power.

I have defined as "theological" an arrangement whereby a domain is unified under "an invisible transcendent sovereign immortal principle." Its rule over those who fall within its domain is total, in a way that creates two very sharp lines of distinction – one between itself and us, and the other between us who belong to it and outsiders. It is bodied-forth in a variety of ways: in a rock that acts as its symbolic focus, in the classic insignia of sovereignty, and perhaps also in a symbolic person who acts as Head of State. Theologies, in the narrow sense of systems of beliefs about gods, are symbolic representations of set-ups of this type. They are ideological, in that they act to "normalize" and validate the relations of domination and subjection that they describe. They explain why it is that you cannot be happy in this life but, if you are a faithful servant, you may attain happiness after death.

In the past, for much of humanity, the State, although on certain highly publicized occasions it could be spectacularly cruel, was for most of the time very inefficient. Religious institutions were usually much more effective as disciplinary instruments. But at the Enlightenment there was a very considerable shift in the balance of power, as the technologies of social administration and control began to improve rapidly. The State became very much more efficient, *so* efficient that it could even afford (partially) to liberalize itself. Religion was now deprived of its coercive powers because they were no longer needed, and even seemed no longer morally tolerable. The result has been that today the State plays the part of God and the Church that of Christ. The State is the all-powerful invisible authority that we can't escape, that rules our lives, that supervises our behaviour in the most minute detail, and that condemns us to a life of subjection to its Law. We know ourselves to be drastically diminished and reduced human beings, and we look to religion for relief and help. The job of religion is to promise salvation, and to appear to be delivering the first instalments of it. But, like entertainers, artists, and social workers, religious professionals are expected and allowed to offer only palliatives and consolations. Their role is to reconcile us to the set-up: they can't change it. They are not permitted to question the deep theological compact that creates the State, the Church, and the unhappy consciousness in the first place. For what dogmatic theology describes as the necessity and the objective reality of God's being is a mythical representation of the melancholy fact – or supposed fact – that human life has to be social life, and social life is possible for us humans only on the basis of strictly enforced common subjection to absolute power and authority.

In Islam, all this is still highly visibly acted out. In the West it has been in various ways moderated and masked – for most of us, at least. But the tragic underlying reality is still the same.

So on the Christian view, there has to be God and there has to be Christ; and we religious professionals are duty bound to insist *both* upon the necessity of human subjection to absolute authority, *and* upon the need to promise, *but never fully to deliver*, salvation from the lifelong unhappy consciousness which is the human lot.

In this way standard Christian doctrine achieves an admirably clear representation of the tragedy of the human condition, a representation which also seeks to reconcile us to it. And that is what I mean by describing dogmatic theology of the sort defined and upheld by the rulers of the Church as an ideology of actual absolute spiritual power – in short, theological realism. Back in the early Iron Age, our religions of redemption at first began with a flight from the State. People fled into mendicancy, into celibacy, into the wilderness, seeking to escape from the savage disciplinary demands and the arrogance of the State. They even sought to escape this world altogether, and find spiritual release in a realm beyond it. But as the religions of redemption settled down in time, and acquired their own power-structures, their motivation shifted. They now preached the inevitability, the necessity, of life under authority, and although they still promised redemption, they situated it at the remote end of a very long and well-policed road.

They preached the message with remarkable success, and to this day most of our contemporaries still accept it all: human beings are wicked, they need to live subject to strong government, religious happiness is not available in this life, and one must accept the authority of a powerful system of religious mediation. As for freedom – we'll never really have *that*, either in this life or the next.

*   *   *   *

God's cosmic sovereignty, as it is represented in theology, has for many millennia given ideological backing to other forms of sovereignty, such as that of universal Reason, that of objective reality, and especially that of the State. This explains why it is that when during the Enlightenment modern atheism began to appear, people simultaneously began to dream of emancipation from the State. For thousands of years human life has been lived under the Law[7] and in a state of subjection to Authority, but now perhaps this ancient servitude might be coming to an end.

A surprising number of lines of political thought converge here: followers of Rousseau, of Marx, and of Nietzsche, anarchists, American rebels against the federal government, and many others too. Voices like these have been muted recently, but now there is again talk of globalization, of the increasing power of international or multinational bodies, and of the relative decline of the sovereign nation-state.

It is against this background that we here invite attention to the currently rather unfashionable literature of mysticism. I shall suggest that the great mystical writers are much more political than at first appears. For the mystic is a religious anarchist and utopian, who speaks for an ancient tradition of protest against religious alienation. The mystic tries to undermine the Law, and to create religious happiness by melting God down – as we shall see.

CHAPTER FOUR

mysticism is a
kind of writing

Here is a very average Englishman of a certain age, describing his early religious quest and its disappointing outcome:

> Like many people who received religious instruction and attended church regularly in their youth, I would have liked to be a believer; I even tried quite hard to be one, but found it impossible. I didn't reject the existence of God or decide to hate Him, like Kingsley Amis – I was too dull and conventional for that – I just couldn't establish any relationship with Him. I would kneel during prayers and screw up my eyes, promising to be a better person, but I felt I was talking to nobody but myself. I was never favoured with a spiritual experience of a wholly convincing kind. So, in the end, I decided it would be ridiculous to pretend to believe.[1]

We have already described this view of religion as being typical of the Modern period – the period intellectually dominated by the rise of natural science. The presumption is that religious beliefs express something like scientific theories. They ought to be verifiable in personal experience. When one has just been confirmed, or married, for example, one hopes to "feel a bit different afterwards," in a way somehow proportionate to what one has been told about the gift in the sacrament of God's Spirit or God's Grace. When one prays or goes to church, when one makes a resolution, again one hopes for some sort of subjectively experienced difference. But there is none. So our average Englishman concludes that he must be religiously tone-deaf or colour-blind (a metaphor that goes back to the eighteenth century in British religious thought). Maybe the highly religious have an extra interior sense-organ that he lacks. Certainly some such philosophy of religion influenced those who in the period around 1840–1970 constructed mystical traditions and canons of mystical writers. In line with the general theory that true sentences somehow copy or describe actually obtaining states of things outside language, it was at that time assumed that mystical texts and personal religious testimonies contain reports in language of extra-ordinary prelinguistic psychological goings-on, which can be taken as furnishing empirical evidence for the truth of at any rate *some* religious beliefs. Most of us would prefer to be granted that kind of confirmation of our faith within our own personal experience; but it doesn't seem to be available. In which case, the testimony of the mystics can be a worthwhile second-best.

It is not easy to make all this more precise, but the best-known attempt to do so is associated with the work of the philosopher W.T. Stace, the author of *Mysticism and Philosophy*[2] and *Time and Eternity*. To help psychologists to investigate and describe religious experiences – mostly of a rather "panenhenic" (from the Greek, *pan en hen*, All-in-One) or pantheistic kind – Stace devised a scale of dimensions or categories, as follows:

1 Unity
   (a) Internal
   (b) External
2 Transcendence of time and space
3 Deeply felt positive mood
   (a) Joy, blessedness, peace
   (b) Love
4 Sacredness
5 Objectivity and reality
6 Paradoxicality
7 Alleged ineffability
8 Transiency
9 Persisting positive changes in attitude and behaviour
   (a) towards self
   (b) towards others
   (c) towards life
   (d) towards the experience.

This scale was accompanied by a set of instructions for assigning numerical values in respect of each of these dimensions. Thus, provided that the subject who claimed to have had the experience was willing to complete a lengthy questionnaire about it, each experience could be given a numerical profile, and differences between one person's experience and another's could be checked against other variables.[3]

Fine: but what exactly is the connection supposed to be between all this and the truth of one or another specific religious or metaphysical belief? Many of the supposed features of mystical experiences are reported in connection with purely secular relaxation exercises and meditation. Thus:

> Deikman (1963) asked eight subjects to meditate on a vase for a series of 15-minute sessions. The subjects all experienced (a) more vivid perception of the vase, e.g. increased colour saturation; (b) personal attachment to the vase; (c) increased ability to keep out distracting stimuli; (d) time shortening; and (e) felt that the experience was pleasant and valuable. Some subjects had more intense experiences, such as seeing the object radiating or transfigured, or a merging of self and object. Meditation was able to generate some of the components of mystical experience.[4]

Today, it should not need saying that a feeling or mood, just as such and prior to its encoding into some philosophical or religious vocabulary, has no meaning and is not an argument. What is it? It may be pleasant or unpleasant, but it doesn't prove anything. Richard Rorty has made the point very well here, by saying that philosophical arguments ought not to include appeal to anything non-propositional. Only by being brought under a *word* can a feeling get a *meaning*, and so become eligible to enter into an argument.

That being so, it is now worth asking whether "the mystics" themselves do in fact supply us with descriptions of "mystical experiences" that they have enjoyed. What sort of people *are* the mystics, and what have they to tell us? Do they in fact report experiences that confirm beliefs?

A glance at a standard work of reference will quickly indicate what sort of people have generally been accounted mystics. For example, *The Oxford Dictionary of the Christian Church* (1958), s.v. "Mysticism") lists 37 names, and the *New Columbia Encyclopaedia* (4th edn, 1975, ibid.) lists some 50 Christian mystics, plus a large number of mystical schools. There are also briefer accounts of the mystical traditions in a number of other faiths.

Both sources given traditional modernist definitions of mysticism: "an immediate knowledge of God attained in this present life through personal religious experience" (*DCC*); "direct relation with God, the Absolute, or any unifying principle of life . . . what he [the mystic] must regard as objective reality immediately perceived" (*NCE*). As befits its more recent date, the *NCE* is a little the more cautious of the two. The very nature of mysticism is such that "firsthand objective studies of it are virtually impossible," and we are in practice dependent upon secondary accounts, autobiographical or biographical. This comes close to admitting that since we must begin in "secondariness," or *writing*, "directness" or "objectivity" is not strictly attainable. So why *write* about it, when the medium must so obviously contradict the message it is trying to convey? But neither the *NCE* nor the *DCC* is able to grasp what today is obvious: their definitions in language of mysticism are self-refuting. They are attempts to say what cannot be said, to eff what is *logically* ineffable. Talk of "direct encounter," seems, *seems*, to conjure up an idea of stepping entirely clear of language, while yet remaining, as it must, firmly embedded within language. We have to give up the non-idea of language's "outside."

Linguistic signs cannot be assembled into combinations such as "objective reality immediately perceived" and "direct encounter with God," without paradox. Perception is a *mediated* relation between the perceiver and the perceived. Linguistic signs are *mediate*. All knowledge is propositional, to such an extent that the very phrase "immediate knowledge" – here marked on this page, a couple of signs, in black and white – looks to be self-refuting twice over. Is it not amazing that even as recently as the 1970s so many scholars still couldn't *think words*?

We can't trick our way out of the difficulty. In English, "I" looks like a minimal, transparent, uncomplicated sign, hardly a sign at all, so that English speakers are perhaps especially ready to be persuaded by Descartes that each of us has an immediate knowledge of her own self. Wrong: even my own knowledge of my own self is never immediate but always mediated, corrigible, disputable, language-dependent. I am my own construct even to myself, and a bit of a botched job too. I don't see myself at all clearly, and often get myself obviously, absurdly wrong. Indeed, I don't know what it would *be* to see myself immediately and with perfect clarity.

In the case of God, just what would it be to see God face to face, to have immediate knowledge of God, to be directly related to God? Please describe the vision of God . . . and of course one cannot, as even John Hick has admitted.[5] The notion that there are or can be, either in mystical rapture or after death, extra-linguistic psychological states or experiences that verify beliefs about God will not bear scrutiny. To *think* it, we'd have to "put it into words," which would drag it down into language. After all, it is supposed to be a state that transcends language: but because all thought depends upon signs, we cannot think ourselves clear of language. Only language can turn an event into an experience *of* something. Looking plus a word equals seeing something; listening plus a word equals hearing something. Language *identifies*, gives meaning. And because we are always in language, we are always in secondariness.

And, in any case, the mystics do not offer us descriptions of language-transcending experiences. If we look at any canonical list of mystics, what one notices straightaway is that these people are *writers*, wordsmiths. Not reporters but *writers*, in the sense of being intellectuals, people highly conscious of language, people who convey their message, not by pointing to something outside language, but by the way they play games *with* language, tormenting it because it torments them, keeping to the rules in such a *wicked* way as to get round the rules. What they write is best interpreted as a slightly mocking and subversive commentary upon the officially approved forms of words for speaking about God. (In the *DCC* list, all 37 persons named wrote; but in several cases it is hard to say how consciously an element of protest enters the writing.) And, furthermore, it is especially noticeable that the proportion of women among mystical writers is everywhere relatively high as compared with the proportion of women writers found working in other literary genres; and it is also noticeable that the proportion of *poets* – especially lyric poets, love poets – is particularly high. In Islam one of the best examples, perhaps, is Rabi'a of Basra (ca. AD 717–801), an ascetic, a poet-saint, and one of the earliest Sufis.[6] Like most, and perhaps all, women mystics she writes a kind of love-poetry that works to subvert the typically male construction of the religious world. Men build a world in which everything is scaled in terms of degrees of presence, power, and rank. The woman mystic subverts these scales by writing with an expressive erotic intensity that sets them aside. So Rabi'a declares that she feels no special reverence for the House of God, and not even for the Ka'ba itself: "It is the Lord of the house whom I need: what have I to do with the house?" Because God is in her heart, she doesn't *need* to turn towards Mecca to pray. She turns to her own outpouring feeling, her heart. The "external" institutions of Islam, made by men for men, tend to exclude women; but the saint by her superior expressive powers is able to sidestep them, and even subvert them, in a way that the men cannot criticize and have to respect. So it is that in her poetry Rabi'a is able sweetly and simultaneously to demolish masculinism, to express the very purest religious devotion, and to write erotic verse – and all without being in the least heterodox even by the men's own standards.

The reason why mysticism not only is but *has* to be a kind of writing is that only in writing, only in secondariness, can one thus do several things at once in such a sweet and disarming way. Do we make the point successfully, here? Secondariness is much more complex and powerful than the old appeal to a primary and founding experience. Mysticism is protest, female eroticism, and piety, all at once, in *writing*. Writing, I say, and not "immediate experience," that Modern fiction. Many or most mystics have been persecuted by the orthodox, but whoever heard of someone being persecuted for *having heretical experiences*? To get yourself persecuted, you have *to publish heretical views*; and at your trial for them your judges will need evidence of them in writing. Indeed, unless mysticism *were* a literary tradition of veiled protest, we'd never have heard of it.

Consider now a stranger, stronger example, the medieval Hindu woman poet-saint who is variously titled Mahādēviyakka or Akkamma. We may call her simply Mahādēvi. She is remembered as one of their founding saints by a Kannada-speaking caste-sect that exists today in the state of Mysore. These people are usually called *Vīraśaivas*, meaning "strict devotees of Siva," or *Lingayats*, because they wear a small stone emblem of Siva, the *linga*. They can trace their origins as far back as the tenth century and the *bhakti* movement, but their own chief early figure was the twelfth-century poet-prophet, Basavanna. He and his associates rebelled against the caste system, its elaborate rituals, and the current temple worship. Their main weapon was their devotional poetry, the *vacanas* through which they expressed their intense personal devotion to Siva:

> The rich
> will make temples for Siva.
> What shall I
> a poor man
> do?
>
> My legs are pillars,
> the body the shrine,
> the head a cupola
> of gold.
>
> Listen, O lord of the meeting rivers [a title of Siva]
> things standing shall fall
> but the moving ever shall stay.
> Basavannah, 820[7]

The ornate medieval temples of South India were built symbolically in the shape of the human body; but like their Christian equivalent in Europe they had become in practice monuments to privilege, hierarchy, and the disproportionately huge wealth and power of a cruelly exploitative ruling class. Basavanna's poem seeks to reverse this corruption of religion by returning the god into his true temple, the living moving human body which is, from the religious point of view, something greater and more enduring than a mere pile of stone.

Basavanna's dates appear to be ca.1106–67 CE. Mahādēvi's short life appears to have been lived entirely within the last twenty-five years or so of his. Almost like a Greek Cynic, Mahādēvi repudiated all social roles, earthly ties and indoor life. Her poetic language and her way of life became entirely outdoor: she was a homeless, wandering poet and devotee of Siva, dressed only in her long hair.

Mahādēvi combines sexual and religious radicalism to a very striking degree. Like so many mystics, she has no special supernatural or philosophical technical terms whatever, and gives no support to the popular-modernist notion that a mystic is a seer who detects goings-on in another, invisible world. On the contrary, Mahādēvi's poetry sticks within the vocabulary and the themes of traditional secular Kannadan love-poetry. Her erotic passion is so consuming that it becomes almost abstract, universal, and objectless. Her "Lord white as jasmine" is everywhere, and everywhere hidden. He undermines all distinctions. It is because he is everywhere that she goes naked in order always to be open to him and ready for him, as the Earth lies open to the sky.[8]

Because her passion is boundless, it will not bear being narrowed down and given form by object-choice, and Mahādēvi therefore rejects the love of men. She says scornfully that in the eyes of her Lord "men, all men, are but women, wives." Whereas from the masculinist point of view of institutional religion, with its carefully marked gradations of rank and power, men are a step nearer to God than are women, from the point of view of mystical religion woman has the natural advantage. The basic religious act of cosmic, total, extravertive self-surrender into bliss is female, and in religious devotion every man has to become a woman – as all men know, including even those who may seem at first sight to be most masculinist in their behaviour. Mahādēvi does indeed have a poem in which she depicts herself as getting some decidedly rough sex from her illicit divine lover:

He bartered [*sic*: "battered"?] my heart,
   looted my flesh,
   claimed as tribute
   my pleasure,
   took over
   all of me.

I'm the woman of love
for my lord, white as Jasmine.
                              Mahādēviyakka, 88

But the readiness to use such language is by no means limited to women. John Donne, like many another male Western Christian, is very ready to assume a female persona and employ just the same imagery on his own account, as he does in the "Holy Sonnet," beginning "Batter my heart, three-person'd God . . .". Donne delights in violent sexual metaphors:

That I may rise, and stand, o'erthrow mee, 'and bend
Your force, to break, blowe, burn and make me new.

And the Sonnet ends:

Take mee to you, imprison mee, for I
Except you'enthrall me, never shall be free,
Nor ever chast, except you ravish mee.
                              (*Poems*, 1633)

Just as much as Mahādēvi, Donne acknowledges the fact that the religious act of unconditional self-surrender into boundlessness undoes, subverts, makes irrelevant the carefully constructed masculine world of boundaries, rules, and scales of value and rank.

But all this is said, done (and undone) by Donne, as by Mahādēvi, in *writing*. Only in writing, in secondariness, can so much be done simultaneously with such clarity and simplicity. We know in fact next to nothing of the historical Mahādēvi. She's legendary. We haven't got her, and we haven't got her "experience." All that survives is a few hundred brief lyric poems and a dialogue – a small body of writing. These texts undermine institutional religion, express cosmic erotic passion, deliver a few heavy blows in the war between the sexes, and give voice to the purest and most intense religious devotion. All at once. In writing. That is mysticism. Art.

> You're like milk
> in water: I cannot tell
> what comes before,
> what after;
> which is the master,
> which the slave;
> what's big,
> what's small.
>   Mahādēviyakka, 11

how mystical
writing produces
religious happiness

Augustine and John of the Cross

According to an ancient and still very influential tradition, our interior and subjective mental life is not dependent upon language. Indeed, thought and language have been thought to move in quite distinct realms. Your mind is inside your skull, upon which language taps from the outside. Words, on this view, are signs used by the external and bodily signalling-apparatus that the mind must employ in order to communicate with other minds. But the words we utter are merely conventional signs which differ from one language to another, and they are at several removes from reality, being – so it is said – merely signs of signs of signs. By contrast, rational thought and its objects are universal, original, and the same in all human beings. Mind is the human being's native endowment, whereas language (though needed, of course) is merely secondary and conventional.

Aristotle makes all these points, in his usual somewhat laboured style:

Words spoken are symbols or signs of affections or impressions of the soul; written words are the signs of words spoken. As writing, so also is speech not the same for all races of men. But the mental affections themselves, of which these words are primarily signs, are the same for the whole of mankind, as are also the objects of which those affections are representations or likenesses . . .[1]

So a written word is the sign of a spoken word, a spoken word is the sign of a thought, and thoughts are signs of their objects – perhaps via "sensible" and "intelligible" forms. Language is a communication-code in which we are trained by society. But our intellectual life as such is free-standing and logically independent of any particular language. We can reason wordlessly, and Aristotle describes truth and falsity as belonging to thoughts before they become by extension properties of sentences.[2] For Aristotle almost as much as for Plato, there is something "theological" about the mind: the life of Reason in us seems to be a participation in the cosmic Objective Reason that runs through everything.

Not only human beings but also spirits may be thought of as participating in this supralinguistic Objective Reason. Dante sees departed souls and angels as being able to communicate with each other purely telepathically. It is not necessary to learn a new language in order to converse with an angel. Disembodied beings are able to "read" each other's minds directly and wordlessly, because thinking is the same in all beings that think, and a disembodied person is all mind, transparent.

This idea of a universal "language of Reason," the same for all rational beings everywhere, has a long history and has taken many forms. Leibniz toyed with the idea of devising a purified and clarified ideal language; a British philosopher, Margaret Masterman, was still working on such a language only a generation ago; and those philosophers of mind who believe that there is thinking which is not in any public and conventional code still sometimes use the word "mentalese" for the supposedly "natural" idiom of thought. Dante may indeed be postulating such a "mentalese" when he finds his own thoughts being read in Paradise:[3] the inhabitants of Heaven being transparent to each other, reading an angel's or a soul's mentalese must have been rather like reading from one of those glass screens used by politicians as they deliver speeches. Perhaps we should picture angels as having bodies of glass?

Embodied beings, however, are *not* transparent to each other. They are opaque, a fact which makes our human languages necessary, and also introduces the possibility of deception. We are hidden inside our bodies, and an external communication-code is needed, to get ideas across from one mind to another. We call our languages "tongues" (Latin, *lingua*; Greek, *glossa*) because it was believed that language began in the mouth of the speaker, and stopped in the ear of the hearer. In my mouth my tongue does the talking: it encodes my thoughts into the appropriate conventional noises, and my breath carries their sound to your ear, where the noises are decoded back into thoughts again. So language runs from the tongue of one person to the ear of another, and writing similarly runs from the hand of one to the eye of another.

Notice, again, that language is seen as being like Morse code. It is external, social, conventional, a regrettable necessity for us who suffer from the handicap of being embodied. By contrast, rationality and mental life are "natural" to us, and not as such dependent upon language at all. *Genesis* pictures Adam as having been a complete, functioning rational man in a state of perfection while still solitary and speechless. Strangely, he seems to invent language by naming the beasts *before* Eve's arrival. Perhaps we are to presume that he taught her to speak *his* tongue.

In retrospect, it must (as I have said) seem to us now that Plato, Aristotle, and the long line of their successors held a highly "theological" view of "the mind" as our participation in a universal order of suprahuman Objective Reason. The mind naturally thinks in the way the universal Logos thinks, and the way God thinks. But some such view of the mind as this has proved quite extraordinarily long-lived. Aristotle's theory is repeated unchanged by John Locke in England over two millennia later: "words, in their primary or immediate signification, stand for nothing but *the ideas in the mind of him that uses them*,"[4] says Locke, meaning that my purpose in speaking to you is to excite in your head the very same ideas that are moving through my own head.

After Locke, things began to change as people began to recognize the immersion of our human life in society and culture. The order was slowly changed, and we came to see language as preceding thought, and the common cultural world as preceding the emergence of individual subjective consciousness. First there was colloquy, then there was soliloquy, and then there was silent individual thought – we have *exactly* reversed the traditional order! The individual mind is no longer seen as being grounded "theologically" in Universal Objective Reason, but as being grounded socially, in the common cultural world of symbolic exchange. But the older tradition has been very tenacious, and it has two important consequences for our present discussion of mysticism and religious experience.

In the first place, the older "theological" conception of mind which was customary before Darwin, before the rise of our late-Modern conception of culture, and before scientific psychology and linguistics – the older conception of mind – still survives, and it helps to explain why people take it so much for granted that they can contact God and the eternal world directly inside their own heads. It is still easy for us, for you and me, to fail to realize how strange this popular belief is – perhaps because we ourselves are still not yet quite free of it. What I have been calling the Modern view of mysticism and religious experience (prevailing, roughly, from Schleiermacher to W.T. Stace, from 1790 to 1970), was in part an expression of nostalgia for a view of the mind that was in fact rapidly slipping away during those same years.

And in the second place, the old view of language as being a mere add-on, external to the mind, conventional, and generally very imperfect helps to explain the still-widespread feeling that language is a medium "inadequate" to express our subjective life satisfactorily. I suggest that ordinary people's belief that they have deep thoughts, intuitions of meanings and truths, and profound experiences all going far beyond what they can put into words – all this is a residue of the old view of mind as being something very great, independent of language and prior to language.

The implications of this for mysticism are well brought out by Augustine in his *Confessions*. In the celebrated conversation with his mother in the garden of the house at Ostia, the two of them seemed to soar higher and higher, beyond the world, beyond the heavens, beyond even their own minds, until momentarily and with a final effort they touched Eternal Wisdom herself:

Then, with a sigh, leaving the first fruits of the Spirit bound to that ecstasy, we returned to the sounds of our own tongue, where the spoken word had both beginning and end.[5]

So they fell back, into ordinary human language. More than almost any other text in the entire classical literature of Christian mysticism, this passage is likely to be called upon to illustrate what I have described as the "Modern" theory of mysticism. The mind transcends language, religious experience goes beyond language, and mystical texts are obliged to torment language in order to *try*, at least, to make it say what cannot be said. The mystical text gropes, gestures, bears witness to something beyond itself, which it cannot capture in its own words. For those who held this view of mysticism, the mystical text was exciting, was tantalizing in an almost erotic way, because of the way it tried to show us something forbidden, something *terribly* alluring that we desperately want to see, but can't.

All this, however, is characteristic only of those texts that set out to describe Plotinian ecstasy[6] and similar states. Furthermore, it is bound up with ideas about the mind and about language that we now see to be wrong and untenable. We need instead an account of mysticism and religious experience that is compatible with our own understanding of language and the mind.

For this, the best starting-point (as I have argued) is surely the observation that most of "the mystics" are highly literary figures. Mystical poetry in particular is polished, literary, and "immanent," or "closed" writing. Whereas Augustine's description of the experience at Ostia tries to use language to point tantalizingly to a transcendent reality that is off the page, the mystical poet has got to produce religious happiness *on the page*, in the writing.

For an example of how this is done, consider the poem by John of the Cross which is called "Song of the Ascent of Mount Carmel." I give below the Spanish text, and a "literal" translation by J.M. Cohen.

Canción de la subida del Monte Carmelo
En una noche oscura,
con ansias en amores inflamada,
¡ oh dichosa ventura!,
salí sin ser notada,
estando ya mi casa sosegada.

A oscuras y segura
por la secreta escala, disfrazada
¡ oh dichosa ventura!,
a oscuras y en celada,
estando ya mi casa sosegada.

En la noche dichoas,
en secreto, que nadie me veía,
ni yo miraba cosa,
sin otra luz y guía
sino la que en el corazón ardía.

Aquesta me guiaba
más cierto que la luz de mediodía,
adonde me esperaba
quien yo bien me sabía
en parte donde nadie parecií.

¡ Oh noche que guiaste,
oh, noche amable más que la alborada,
oh, noche que juntaste
Amado com Amada,
Amada en el Amado transformada!

En mi pecho florido,
que entero para él sólo se guardaba,
allí quedó dormido,
y yo le regalaba
y el ventalle de cedros aire daba.

El aire del almena,
cuando ya sus cabellos esparcía,
com su mano serena
en mi cuello hería
y todos mis sentidos suspendía.

Quedéme y olvidéme,
el rostro recliné sobre el Amado,
cesó todo, y dejéme,
dejando mi cuidado
entre las azucenas olvidado.

Song of the Ascent of Mount Carmel

1   In a dark night, inflamed by love's desires – oh, lucky chance! – I went out unnoticed, all being then quiet in my house.

2   In darkness and safe, by the secret staircase, and disguised – oh, lucky chance! – in darkness and by stealth, all being then quiet in my house.

3   On that lucky night, in secret, since no one saw me nor did I see anything, with no other light or guide except the light that was burning in my heart.

4   This guided me more certainly than the light of midday, to where one awaited me whom I knew well, in a place where no one was to be seen.

5   Oh, night that was the guide; oh, night more delightful than the dawn; oh, night that joined Lover with Mistress, the Mistress transformed into the Lover!

6   In my burgeoning heart, which kept itself wholly for him alone, here he stayed asleep, and I entertained him, and the cedars were the fan that made the breeze.

7   The wind from the battlements, as it scattered his hair, wounded me on the neck with its smooth hand, and suspended all my senses.

8   I remained and forgot myself, I laid my face against the Lover, everything stopped and left me, leaving my cares forgotten among the lilies.[7]

As we saw, Augustine's passage describing the experience in the garden of Ostia lends itself to being read in the Modern way as an autobiographical testimony, in which he recalls and tries to describe, in words, a great personal experience of something beyond words. I have my own doubts about that, because the text is in a form that *itself* has a literary history: it is an account of Plotinian ecstasy. It is derived from the *Enneads* of Plotinus

(6.9.11.23), which in turn is itself indebted to earlier Platonists such as Philo of Alexandria. Augustine is not in fact describing an extra-linguistic experience; he is merely rewriting an earlier bit of writing. But let that point stand: as we turn now to John of the Cross it is clear that he gives us no kind of witness-statement. It is a highly polished poem that is the product of a long and complex literary tradition. It demands detailed *literary* analysis to show what it says and how it works. It is true that John has also written a mystical treatise on "The Ascent of Mount Carmel," but it is to be noticed that the treatise came second and is in the form of a commentary on the poem. The poem came first; *it* is the starting-point, and not some putative "experience."

The theory of mysticism that I am proposing should now be clearly in view. According to the Modern view of mysticism, as we have seen, the mystics first had great and ineffable experiences, in states of consciousness that were prior to and outside language, and then they subsequently tried to put into inadequate words what they had experienced.

I reject that theory. There is no such thing as "experience," outside of and prior to language. The Modern idea of the mind as an inner theatre, and of experience as a show seen by an audience of one, is itself a secondary cultural and literary creation. It doesn't exist! Language goes all the way down. Language doesn't copy or convey experience; language determines or forms experience as such. Language "forms" certain events, and thereby makes them into conscious experiences. Language *is* mind: I mean, what we call "the mind" is secondary; it is an effect of language. St John of the Cross did not first have a language-transcending experience and then subsequently try to put it into words. On the contrary, the very composition of the poem was *itself* the mystical experience. The happiness is *in the text*; it lies in the fact that John, in prison, has been able through the imagery of the poem to make religious happiness out of the various conflicting forces bearing upon him and the personal suffering that he is undergoing. *Writing* is redemption; religious experience is self-expression in religious art. Mysticism is mystical writing: that is, it is writing and only writing that reconciles conflicting forces and turns suffering into happiness. A person "has a religious experience" when she is able through religious imagery or ritual to "get herself together," and to experience the harmonization and reconciliation of the various forces bearing upon her and within her.

Conflicting Forces

Some commentators on the dark-night poem have insisted that it not only *can* be read but *should* be read simply as a human love-song. Nothing actually in the poem, they have said, obliges the reader to give it a religious interpretation. In this respect John's poem is in the same situation as the love-songs in the *Song of Songs* in the Bible, upon which it is modelled. It is now generally agreed that the *Songs* probably originated as lyrics of human love, and many biblical critics would emphasize the value of reading them simply as such. But when they were highly praised by the rabbis (including even Akiba himself) and retained in the Hebrew canon of scripture, they were taken into a religious context where, for example, prophets like Hosea, Jeremiah, and Ezekiel had already modelled the relation of Israel to her God on the relation of a bride to her husband. In addition, many or most of the lyrics in the *Song of Songs* are written from the woman's point of view, which made it all the easier for the later Christian mystical tradition to appropriate them. But the fact remains that the lyrics are best read as straight secular love-songs which just happened to get incorporated into Scripture and were read for almost two millennia as religious allegories. St John of the Cross, standing in that long tradition, also writes a straight lyric of human love, to which he appends a treatise (unfinished, in fact) reading it as a mystical allegory. It is known that the Spanish literature of that period delighted in a very close parallelism between sacred and profane love: one might, for example, use the same word *ayuntamiento* both for sexual union and for mystical union.[8] So one might take an entirely serious religious pleasure in the *double entendre*, writing in a way that simultaneously keeps the allegory going and keeps the two readings distinct.

All this is very intriguing, because so many comic-opera plots might by the same argument be interpreted as profound allegories of the spiritual life. The commonest plot-type of all has a heroine who is a young maiden (*soprano*), in the guardianship of her Father, an old man (*bass*). He is benevolent, and we never doubt that he does intend her ultimate happiness, but he insists for the present on guarding her virtue. The happiness she ardently longs for must be deferred. She must live under strict supervision, under discipline, even in a sort of semi-confinement, watched over by a Mother-figure (*contralto*) who acts as her Father's agent and her duenna, her chaperone, guarding her, keeping her pure. How is the poor girl ever to be able to meet her Lover (*tenor*)? Fortunately, she has a confidante, a maid, a confessor (*baritone*) even, who suggests that it may be possible to slip away unobserved to a nocturnal rendezvous with her Lover.

And so on: this standard comic-opera situation is beginning to look like a minutely detailed allegory of the human soul under Catholicism. The heroine is the human soul, her father is God the Father, who insists upon deferring the consummation that he nevertheless truly intends for her and has promised. The Mother-duenna is the Church or Mary. The confidante is the spiritual director, and the Lover is Christ, the soul's affianced. The nocturnal rendezvous is long familiar from the myth of Eros and Psyche in Apuleius, from the *Song of Songs* (3:1–4), from John's own dark-night poem, and so on.

Now we ask: when we see a comic opera with such a plot; when we see obstacles overcome, happiness attained, and in the end all the characters reconciled – *why are we not conscious of having a religious experience?* If John's poem gives us a feeling of religious happiness, why doesn't the comic opera that tells the same story?

The answer lies in one word of the poem, *transformada*. In sixteenth-century Spanish writing about love there is a suggestion that neither human sexual love nor divine mystical passion can wholly achieve the union that they long for.[9] In the case of human sexual love, the sensuousness and embodiedness, the sheer sexy Otherness that makes us desire union with the

Beloved also prevents us from attaining it completely and per-manently. We cannot be wholly fused together: we remain two, we must draw apart, and one day one of us will be condemned to survive the other. We therefore cannot be perfectly united for ever. Our love is tragic, an impossible project. Even at its highest and most intense, human love is haunted by anguish; but so, still more, is divine love. In the *Cantico espiritual* John sends God a message: "I am ill, I suffer, I am dying." A.A. Parker explains that "traditionally the human soul had three powers, memory, understanding and will, and each suffers by having no direct experience of God, each in a way appropriate to its func-tion."[10] And he explains in a footnote:

> Knowledge of the truth is the health of the mind; the under-standing is therefore ill if it does not know him. The will's func-tion is to love the good and to possess it; possession of the good brings pleasure and delight, as in love; without the God whom it loves but does not possess the will therefore suffers. Memory only remembers that it has never known God nor possessed him; since God is the promise of life the memory that he is lacking is tantamount to death.[11]

Thus it was a commonplace in John's time that neither human love nor divine can achieve the consummation that they long for. In neither case can one be completely merged into and fused with the Other. In human love, we remain two persons, two bodies. In divine love the infinite ontological difference between the creature and the omnipresent Creator means that, although we already coincide with God and are as close to God as we could conceivably be, God remains hidden from the mind. Thus it is true at once that we couldn't be closer to God and that we couldn't be farther from God, a paradox, a tragic con-tradiction, that seems to be metaphysically incurable.

Returning now to St John's poem, one notices that the first four stanzas are entirely concerned with emphasizing the solitary, nocturnal, clandestine, illicit nature of the enterprise on which the poet is engaged. In stanza five the lovers meet, and the poet's assumption of a female persona is declared. Their union brings about a kind of mutual indwelling: he gives himself into her, and she is "transformed" into him. In the commentary-treatise on the poem, John even says that the one who loves God in the end "becomes God." He justifies this extreme language by quoting the old Augustinian maxim that everyone tends to become what he loves most.[12] A state of serene and apparently unending bliss then follows.

The commentators explain the emphasis on the soul's solitary nocturnal journey into God in terms of the need to put off the body and the senses, and empty oneself of every earthly attachment. Very well: but why is there something *illicit* about the whole enterprise? It must be, it can only be, that John knows very well that his journey is a journey into what the standard dogmatic theology will regard as deadly heresy. Mystical writing is by its nature very dangerous. The mystic knows that the soul can only be eternally happy in God if the God–Man disjunction is overcome, but how can one say so? Religious happiness is wrong; it is heresy to teach its attainability. John has to write in such a way as to insinuate his heresy while maintaining what political advisors nowadays call "plausible deniability."

The heresy is the heresy of teaching deification (= Greek, *apotheosis*). A creature may not claim to have become its Creator. The saints in glory are still only human beings, and any claim to have become more than human must attract grave suspicion. But in that case what do we make of the word "transformation"? John gets his "plausible deniability" from the fact that the word is used in Scripture, quite innocuously, by St Paul at *Romans* 12:3 (Greek *metamorphosis* being the standard equivalent of the Latin *transformation*). But John also insinuates his heresy through his echo of *Philippians* 2:5ff., where Christ's own and proper form is the form of God.

John of the Cross in prison, then, has written a poem that does several jobs at once. It is a kind of protest against the cruelty of ecclesiastical power and ecclesiastical factionalism. It is an affirmation of religious victory and religious happiness. It claims to have overcome the problem of love's permanent suffering and anxiety, and if it thereby runs close to claiming "deification," the claim is advanced only with plausible deniability.

And this many-leveled complex job is the sort of job that only writing can do. Did anybody ever suppose that "direct personal experience," whatever that is supposed to be, could be capable of fixing something so delicate? In order to achieve the perfect religious happiness that standard Christian theology seems to promise but in fact coldly forbids, John must write in a way that destabilizes, and even brings about the final collapse, of that same standard theology. John's text creates an effect of great religious happiness where the comic opera doesn't, because John's in it for real. He knows and we know that he must insinuate religious happiness through a complex, deniable *double entendre*. He is giving us a forbidden pleasure, with even a suggestion that in religion as in sex the fruit tastes all the sweeter for being forbidden. That is the truth: but in the circumstances of John's life it was a truth that could be conveyed only with the help of a great deal of literary art.

the politics
of mysticism

On 1 June 1310 an array of civic and ecclesiastical dignitaries gathered in what is now the Place de l'Hôtel de Ville, Paris, to watch Marguerite Porete being burnt alive. She was a Béguine from Hainault in northern France, and the author of a popular mystical treatise called *The Mirror of Simple Annihilated Souls who dwell only in the Wishing and Desire of Love*. It shows her to have been an early teacher of the doctrine of Pure Love. In her ideas about Being and God she may be less dazzling than her contemporary Eckhart, and in her ideas about disinterested love she does not go to such extremes as the later Quietists; but her teaching does have its own distinctive flavour and quality. She refused to recant, and was condemned by the theologians of the University of Paris. Her book survived, however, and was translated into many European languages. It is even said to have influenced the early Quakers.[1]

A case like this one of Marguerite Porete raises the question of why mystical writings were felt by the authorities to be so very threatening and dangerous. Why did leading churchmen feel it necessary to execute saintly people by public burning? In all periods before the twentieth century mystics have been liable to attract suspicion, but there have been times when they have suffered from something close to witch-hunting. Spain in the 1550s to 1570s is an example. Great figures such as Luis de Leon and John of the Cross were severely persecuted, mystical writings were put on the Inquisition's Index of prohibited books, and contemplative prayer *as such* was regarded as suspect.[2] So great was the fear of passive contemplation and Pure Love that in effect all prayer was supposed to be directly linked to human self-improvement and resolutions about one's conduct.

In this connection, K.E. Kirk describes the well-known Jesuit writer Alphonso Rodriguez being cautious: "The Christian must never have more than *one eye* fixed upon God – the other must be sternly and critically gazing at himself." In Rodriguez' own words:

> Whilst therefore we have one eye engaged in contemplating God, we must engage the other in seeing how to do all things well for his love, so that consideration of being in his presence may be a means to oblige us to do all our actions better.[3]

At the height of a period of anti-mystical fury, one might say, the Church Militant reveals a deep commitment to military and masculinist values: the will, self-discipline, obedience, resolution, spiritual warfare. In the early parts of the Hebrew Bible, as in Islam and Sikhism, the religious community becomes an army of male warriors whose God marches to battle at their head; while monks have turned into soldiers not only in Latin Christianity, but also in Japanese Buddhism. Everywhere it is held that warfare demands ritual purity: deferred happiness, strict discipline, unconditional loyalty, and a clear chain of command. At the opposite extreme the typically mystical movement, the soul's passive self-surrender into bliss, is regarded with horror. It is lazy, damp, female, and self-indulgent. It is highly heretical because it blurs boundaries: above all, because it blurs the most important boundary there is, that between the Creator and his creature.

St Ignatius Loyola was himself very much a soldier of Christ, and his prayers were Spiritual "Exercises" or, as the Salvation Army used to say, "knee drill." He was surely irreproachably masculinist and authoritarian. Yet such was the climate created by the notorious Dominican Melchior Cano that even the Jesuits quaked, and Mercurian their General in 1573 banished practically every known mystical writing from Jesuit libraries. In the following decades it was made clear that Jesuits pray in order to improve their self-mastery and their moral will. Prayer is "an instrument of acquiring and exercising virtue";[4] it is a way of tightening oneself up, not a way of release. Only strenuousness is good: religious happiness is bad, even disgusting and dangerous.

We have already suggested that there is here an example of a conflict that runs right through the history of Western Christianity, and has parallels in other traditions too.

The dominant, ruling-class ethos is institutional, priestly, and patriarchal. Its mind is expressed in the machinery by which religious law is produced and enforced, and in dogmatic theology. This tradition, the tradition of "the Fathers," is highly masculinist. The Cosmos, the religious society and the human self are all seen in terms of power and control. Religious happiness and fulfilment are deferred into the very-long-term future, at the end of history or after death. In the meanwhile, the model believer battles for mastery and self-mastery, and seeks to strengthen the System. He wants to see a stable institutional life, with orderly routines and carefully marked gradations of rank. Happiness can wait.

Increasingly under such a set-up the System becomes an end in itself and ritual becomes, like a ceremonial parade, its own symbolic self-celebration. In the old ceremonies of the Latin Rite, for example, the Mass was in effect the System's self-representation. The step you stood on, the vestments you wore, the number of times you bowed, the number of swings of the censer, the number of jingles of the bell, the orchestration of movements – everything spoke of what is, to older males at least, the most interesting thing in the world: a disciplined spiritual power-structure. Both the Church and the Cosmos are seen as ordered pyramids of power and authority, and the ecclesiastical hierarchy closely parallels the celestial. The Church is like a mighty army: as my drill-sergeant used to say (or rather, to shriek), "You're not paid to think!" – but you *are* told what to believe and how you fit into the System, which is all you need to know.

The other tradition is the opposite of all this in almost every imaginable respect. It is a tradition of protest. It is irregular and charismatic, not institutional; it is often lay rather than clerical, and its imagery is almost entirely feminine rather than masculine. Its typical literary idiom is not Law but poetry, and its outlook is short-termist rather than long-termist. It seeks personal religious happiness, not by setting up clear distinctions, but rather by dissolving them. It does not speak about the will, discipline, and good order, but about love, self-surrender, and resting in God.

The two traditions began to be conscious of themselves and of their differences in the second century CE, when the "Urcatholicism" of episcopal government, baptismal creeds, synods and Church law began to emerge and to battle against the various less institutionally ordered forms of belief that it came to describe as being "Gnostic" and otherwise "heretical."

Then in more recent times the conflict has taken the form of a struggle between *dogmatic theology*, which is chiefly interested in questions of law, discipline, and community belief, and the *mystical theology* that has been produced by writers whose chief interest is in the individual's quest for personal religious happiness. I have been suggesting that the mystical tradition represents a protest against the legalism of the dogmatic tradition, its obsession with power and control, and its consequent failure – even refusal – to deliver the personal salvation that it seems to promise. Mystical writing may be seen as attempting to deconstruct at least some of the great distinctions established by dogmatic theology, and especially the dogmatic ideas of God, the human self, and the infinite qualitative difference between them.

From this point of view we now have an explanation of the persecution of the mystics. As men see it – and perhaps as society generally sees it – the task of religion is to structure the world, setting up clear categories, distinctions, and boundaries, and laying down rules accordingly. One remains ritually clean as long as one respects these things.[5] Woman's misfortune, however, is that she is much more liable than Man to blur the distinctions and to contract ceremonial uncleanness. Her body's boundaries are less clear-cut, and her physical life is more interwoven with other life. She tends to blur together her many and various loves, in a way that Man thinks he cannot and must not do.

So: Man distinguishes, Woman unites. Man sets up the great distinctions, Woman tends always to undermine them, and she is therefore apt to be regarded with horror. In religion, the politically dominant tradition, institutional and masculinist, fights to establish and control doctrinal and ritual boundaries and distinctions. The ideal Christian is a male celibate, and the next best is a female celibate. One needs a dry, clean, and disciplined body with no polluting discharges. From the point of view of this tradition God has to be so Top Brass as to be permanently out of sight, and mysticism is regarded with horror as undermining due order. It is unclean, improper, and polluting. It is female.

Notice in this connection the reason why the religious authorities traditionally regarded the only really acceptable woman as Woman *minus* her own femaleness, celibate woman, the perpetual-*Virgin* mother. It appears that a certain misogynistic horror of female sexuality has in the past played a very large part in the constitution of religious worlds and the construction of religious systems of thought. For example, people still say unthinkingly that "God made us," attributing our existence to a masculine God who cannot possibly be thought of as having a feminine consort: and they seem quite unaware of their own seeming denial of human motherhood.

Some further explanation is called for here. Simone de Beauvoir's celebrated dictum that one is not born but made a woman seems to suggest that the pressure upon girl children to conform to the current cultural stereotype of Woman is greater, much greater, than the pressure upon a boy child to become and be a man. De Beauvoir seems to be saying that a woman is more the victim of pressure to conform to a cultural ideal than a man is.

I disagree. Is it not the case that a man who failed to be and to do what is required of men by men was far more severely punished (by his fellow men) than a woman who failed to be and to do what was required of women? Male homosexuality – and especially *passive* male homosexuality – was traditionally regarded as being much more disgraceful and even criminal than lesbianism, and like cowardice in battle was punishable by death. Lesbianism by contrast was treated so indulgently as to be overlooked altogether until quite recent times.

In many or most societies male and female children are at first raised together. But there comes a moment, around the age of eight or so, when a boy child must distance himself from the world of women. His hair is cut, he is put into masculine dress such as a sailor suit, and he is taken into a more masculine world. Henceforth he must spend much of his life competing with men in the world of men, and meeting the demands of men, and a certain sexual segregation is enforced. It is bad for a man to be too uxorious, bad for a woman to come aboard a working boat or down a coal-pit, and impossible for a woman to become a priest alongside men. Men must keep their distance, the distance that makes them men.

Such ideas were hugely powerful in the cultural world we are now at last leaving behind. One might say that in traditional thought the act by which Man becomes Man and remains Man, by distancing himself a little from the world of women, was the fundamental model for the relations of culture to nature, of reason to feeling, and of spirit to flesh. In certain respects Man has to be more disciplined than Woman. Man must harden himself, and say No for a while to comfort, ease, and pleasure. He must concern himself with war, and with the establishment of order, hierarchy, law, government, dominion. He will tend to perceive Woman as a seductress, a temptress, whose blandishments threaten to distract and weaken him from his proper concerns.

Men's myths repeat these themes. Enkidu is fatally weakened by the harlot, and Samson (who is presumably Shemesh the sun-god, whose strength is in his rays, his hair) is fatally weakened by Delilah. By contrast, Christ does not become compromised. He gracefully recoils from Mary Magdalen: "Touch me not"; and his priests must similarly maintain their proper distance from women in order to preserve their mystique.

Against this background one can perhaps imagine why people should have supposed that God, who is in a sense the super-male, must likewise keep his proper distance from the human soul. The orthodox could accept that the human soul must cast itself as female, and endeavour almost to *seduce* God; but it was axiomatic that, because God is pure and infinite spirit, the infinite qualitative difference between God and the human soul must always be maintained and cannot be breached or blurred; not even in the Beatific Vision, and not even in the Incarnation. Any mystic who claimed to have violated the difference, and to have "become" God, was a blasphemer who deserved death.

The dogmatic tradition, then, has always perceived the mystical tradition as female and therefore as potentially unclean and threatening. Hence the bizarre ferocity with which mystics have been persecuted. But the mystical tradition could not be wholly extinguished: because a female element enters into the constitution of men as well as women, men have always found it very easy and congenial to cast themselves as women in their relation to God. In her works of feminist theology, Daphne Hampson refers rather disparagingly to this fact;[6] but the present argument is that it is highly significant. Men are the children of women just as women are: the female principle is just as much constitutive as men as it is of women (not least because a man has one female parent and one male parent, exactly as a woman has), and although most men have tended to repress the female element within themselves much more than most women do, they nevertheless do like to give it an airing, especially in religion and art. Most men enjoy a holiday from military discipline, self-mastery, and alienation. So men may be as much attracted to mysticism as women are, and it is amusing to see with what relief and relish the most masculinist man may in his devotions use the language and express the feelings of a woman.

Thus the mystical tradition has almost always existed (at least until as late as St Thérèse of Lisieux, who died on September 30, 1897),[7] and it is their mystical traditions that could yet be the saving of Islam and Christianity. But of course the mystical tradition was never dominant. It was always only a compensation, a protest, and a corrective. In the developed metaphysical theology of Christendom and Islam the gulf between God and the human self appears absolute and unbridgeable. Infinite, and infinitely alien, spiritual power is omnipresent, and therefore bears upon me at every point of my being. It is hidden from me just by the deep darkness of its own infinite difference. The idea is horrifying. In the Pure-Love and the Quietist traditions of writing, the gulf is overcome chiefly by progressively emptying the human self and so writing it out of the script. The human self is stripped, and voided of everything but its own yearning for God. As the self abandons itself completely to God, it becomes a vacuum into which God rushes – but without changing, because God is everything everywhere already. Happiness is achieved, then, by the self's literary self-annihilation, which leaves only God. This literary suicide bears witness to God's greatness and the greatness of the soul's love for him. The subtext is that it also solves the problem of the metaphysical horror that the idea of God arouses in us.

We now grasp that there are several ways in which one may seek to overcome religious alienation and write religious happiness by undermining the classic metaphysical disjunction between the self and God. Marguerite Porete's ascetical style writes away the self, emptying it until it is nothing but a vacuum into which God rushes. John of the Cross creates religious happiness by writing the soul's spiritual marriage with God, a union so intimate that the beloved soul finds herself transformed into the Lover. Spinoza, Shankara, and other non-dualists Eastern and Western create religious happiness by making the human self merely a mode of the One universal divine reality. Here the philosophical proof of monism is also a writing of redemption. Finally, and fourthly, Buddhism begins with a liberating philosophical attack on the self.

Man distinguishes, Woman unites. The "masculine" principle, interested in establishing and governing a well-ordered world, likes to have things cut-and-dried: binary oppositions, clear categories and gradations, and firm lines separating right from wrong, the permitted from the forbidden, and the clean from the unclean. The "feminine" principle, interested in happiness, is a protest and a corrective that works to undo and reconcile. But I am speaking of ideal types or principles, rather than about actual human beings, who may appear to contain within themselves very varied mixes of these principles. For example, it is easy for such Western Christian writers as Augustine and Bernard to be great churchmen, highly ruling-class and "masculinist," keen on power and persecution – who yet, when they are in their mystical vein, become entirely and convincingly "feminine." Conversely, among women intellectuals it is quite common to meet people who are firmly heterosexual, but highly masculinist in their thinking.

Now a question arises about the origin of these two styles of thinking, and the conflict between them in the religious tradition. As we have seen already, both in the State and in institutional religion it has been assumed for several millennia that the human condition is – and needs to remain – unhappy. Human beings are very wayward; they need to be disciplined and subjected to firm government. In fact, it has been normal to think that for the whole of our lives, both in religion and in civil society, we human beings must live in a condition of subjection to absolute legislative Power. It follows that religious alienation is "normal" and appropriate for human beings: at least, it is the condition in which we all begin, and whose final overcoming we shall not see in this life. As long as we live, the Power that rules us will be set *over* us. And *over* means over *against*: in order to make a nomad into a citizen you have to put the fear of a god into him. You have to reduce him to such a state of metaphysical horror that he will be very ready to give up his life when required to do so.

Today virtually all living human beings are citizens of State societies. We live all our lives in a condition of subjection to what is still in effect an absolute monarch, a sovereign legislative Authority that has the power of life and death over us and that regulates our lives minutely. It may conscript us into the armed forces and send us off to mass slaughter in war, for example; and since this particular power of the sovereign or the State has hitherto borne down chiefly upon males, the whole business of law and government has in the past been chiefly the concern of men. Males have had the larger and more direct investment in the System, both the political system and the ecclesiastical system, and both for good and ill. It has been males who have understood most clearly the three propositions:

1   That human nature, or the human condition, is radically unsatisfactory.
2   That human beings must therefore live under discipline in a state of subjection to a great and commanding public Authority.
3   That religious alienation is therefore our lot in this life.

A consequence of these assumptions is that human beings are not fit for moral autonomy, and in this life never will be. So in the book of *Judges* the ancient Israelite historian has a set formula to explain really deplorable behaviour: "In those days there was no king in Israel; every man did what was right in his own eyes."[8] Three millennia later this is probably still the majority view, even in self-styled "free" countries. Men need to be bridled like animals. Freedom unbridled is licentiousness, libertinism.

It is in this area, I am suggesting, that we should seek the origins of the "dogmatic" tradition of the Fathers and the Law, and an understanding of its association with men and "masculinist" values. For historical reasons, men have been more inclined than women to see the advantages of common subjection to discipline. It wins battles: it strengthens both the Church and the State. As for the contrary tradition, the mystical tradition, the tradition of utopian protest that declines to accept lifelong religious alienation, I suggested earlier (p. 56) that we may see it as related not only to lay and feminine values, but also to anarchism in politics. Anarchists tend also to be atheists: "Why *should* everyone live their entire life under discipline and in a state of subjection to Authority?," they ask.

Although in the past there have been lively versions of anarchism both on the political right and on the political left, and in countries as diverse as England, Spain, and the USA, anarchism has seldom attracted serious intellectual attention for long. This may change, however, as we become more widely aware of the rapid decline of the sovereign nation-state. During the twentieth century we have seen many or most of the old consanguineous nation-states transformed into multi-ethnic societies, and although we still hear our politicians talking about "the nation" and its sovereignty, we are aware that their rhetoric is increasingly at odds with the manifest facts. The British courts – for example – now yield precedence at many points to the European courts of justice and human rights; Britain is signed up as a member of innumerable international organizations that prescribe standards and whose decisions we are pledged to respect; British troops have long been held more-or-less permanently under foreign command in NATO; and large sectors of the economy are presently in foreign ownership. Finance, communications, the English language, culture, and indeed knowledge are increasingly globalized. One might say that a world-wide-web of "horizontal" agreements and systems of exchange is already rapidly replacing the old sovereign State in which everything came to a focus in and depended upon a single central controlling sovereign Power. Thus although constitutionally Britain remains nominally a mon-*arche*, the reality is increasingly an-*arche*, the condition of being without a superior founding, unifying, and governing Principle; and the same is true of other countries also.

Because we are emotionally still monarchists in politics, realistic theists in religion, and foundationalists (Cartesians, usually) in philosophy, anarchy has a dirty name. It is a Yeatsian nightmare: "Mere anarchy is loosed upon the world." But in fact anarchy can turn out to be far more powerful and efficacious than absolute monarchy. For example: What makes and keeps the English language as hugely flexible and alive as it is? Is there a great policeman in the sky whose Will holds all the meanings of English words in place, and whose Intellect has foreordained all the proper constructions? Does language need an *arche* or founding Principle? No: of course it does not. All that is needed to keep English alive and powerful is the interest that each and every one of us has in using it effectively in the billions of exchanges about matters small and great that take place daily around the world.

That's all. It's mere anarchy; but it is far more powerful than any linguistic monarch could hope to be, rather as Richard Dawkins' myriad detailed Darwinian stories[9] about how and why living things have come to be the way they are is *by far* more interesting and powerful than the other sort of explanation that merely referred everything to Special Creation by a divine and all-powerful *Arche*.

The purely immanent interest each organism has in surviving, and that each human being or group has in communicating effectively, is now well known to be a highly effective discipline. It is an *immanent* discipline. We need to grasp Darwin's paradox, that Natural Selection, with *no* external selector, is very much more effective and flexible than Artificial Selection by an external Selector who is making the choices with a view to the fulfilment of his own purposes. When we grasp this we see that there is no reason to fear anarchy and radical immanence. Far from it, because the surviving absolute monarchies, theocratic societies, and other sorts of dictatorship are without exception in our experience backward, cruel, and corrupt. When did people's desire for a "strong leader" ever do them any good? Doesn't it now look as if a fully horizontalized world might be much more rational and peaceful, and much less self-destructive? Instead of trusting Authority, why not try trusting conversation, democracy, and bargaining?

If we can begin to imagine a fully horizontalized world without any remaining centres of absolute power and authority, in either Church or State; if we can imagine trusting our daily worldwide processes of exchange to produce reality, keep order, and sustain values without any Outside underpinning or direction – then we can perhaps imagine an anarchist world. It would be a post-metaphysical world in which everything is immanent, everything is at one level, everything is relative or secondary. It would be a world in which the divine is seen as having become dispersed into individual persons, a radically democratic world without distinctions of rank, oaths of obedience, or the use of coercive force by Authority. In short, it would be the sort of social world to which the Society of Friends has been bearing witness since the year 1668.

We are so habituated to the idea that "the mystics" were solitary individuals, absorbed in their own inner lives, that my suggestion that mysticism is political may come as a surprise. But the Society of Friends is an excellent and still flourishing example of a mystical society which has always been clear about the ethical and political implications of the mystical critique, both of orthodox religion and of political sovereignty. And more recently the American Cistercian Thomas Merton (1915–68) became in his later years increasingly aware of the connections between mysticism and politics.

Are these ideas far-fetched? We live at a time of the un-rivalled global dominance of capitalism. Socialism is in eclipse, and it is not easy to see what force can limit and counterbalance the destructive effects of the marketization of all life. I suggest that the tools we need are to be found in the mystical tradition, with its concern for happiness and its long-practiced skills in writing against and around the domination of life by a single truth-power.

CHAPTER SEVEN

mystical writing was the forerunner of deconstruction and radical theology

I have been suggesting that we are currently in process of giving up all the many forms of the ancient "theological" belief that the here-and-now cannot stand on its own and needs to be supported, grounded, supervised, and directed from a point outside it. We are accustoming ourselves to the idea that even though everything in the world of experience is indeed only fleeting and contingent, still, it can look after itself. A purely immanent vision of things is possible: we no more need to suppose that some sort of eternal world undergirds this world than we need to suppose that the Earth has to be supported upon the shoulders of the giant Atlas.

The philosophical shift being made here is not easy, but in a number of areas we have already made it. In democratic politics, for example, we are surely happy to live with the idea that final truth is never reached. In democratic societies everything is contingent and negotiable, and nothing is sacrosanct. Political life is an unending debate, and a perfect state of society and of the law is a receding ideal, never actually realized. The current state of the law approximately reflects the current consensus, and like a dictionary reveals many deposited traces of past controversies and debates. But we have no extra-historical yardstick against which to measure whether or not the whole body of law is now "better" than it was at some stage – *and we do not need one!* We have found that there can perfectly well be morality without either moral progress or moral perfection. We don't *have* to describe moral change as being either for the better or for the worse. There is no objective moral order, and no ready-made ruler to measure moralities with. Our morality is historically evolved, improvised, and untidy. We can make rational judgements about it, and we can try to change it; but we cannot and we should not pretend to be able to assign relative grades to various moralities as if from an absolute standpoint.

Democratic political life and debate is an excellent example – perhaps it is the prime example – of what some people nowadays refer to disparagingly as "relativism." Such people often say or imply that "moral relativism" is morally weak and not strong enough to stand, and they may go on to speak with admiration of "absolutes" and "strong leadership." They seem to hanker after a powerful external Authority who knows all the Law – perhaps *is* the Law – and can uphold the moral order. But surely experience suggests rather that consistently democratic societies are likely to be strong and morally healthy, whereas the theocracies, the absolute monarchies and the dictatorships are almost invariably corrupt and weak. (If you doubt me, I challenge you to name a virtuous theocracy extant today.) It seems that a purely immanent politics, with no higher authority than a fluid, shifting public consensus, succeeds better than any number of "absolutes" and "objective truths."

By parallel reasoning (as I have already suggested, above) we are gradually learning that it is best to allow our language – the first, the greatest, and the most valuable of our cultural possessions – to evolve democratically and unpoliced. In Greece, in France, and elsewhere there have been attempts by national academies to limit and to control the course of linguistic change. Such attempts have had little effect. English does better, although it is notoriously irregular and is unpoliced.

Language looks after itself: an unregulated free market is best. Similarly, Darwinian Natural Selection without any external Selector proves well able to generate a marvellously rich and varied tapestry of life. The species it produces are surely more robust, vital, and adaptable than those produced by plant and animal breeders.

The general lesson to be learnt from these and many other examples that might be quoted is that we really *can* now give up every sort of teleology, rationalism, and foundationalism. We do not need to suppose that everything is held together by serving some great external Purpose. We can do entirely without suprahuman fixed Standards. We do not need to suppose that threads of logical necessity run through everything and hold the world together. And we do not need to suppose that the changing world is supported by an unchanging World-Ground. There is no First Principle; everything is secondary. Just the streaming, purely contingent flux of things, unpoliced, is well able to generate natural languages, values, organisms, and human societies. Relativity is creativity; the world is just *play*. The mysticism of secondariness accepts universal pure contingency, goes with the flow, and trusts the processes of life spontaneously to generate form and meaning. Let it come. And – it does! The world is created, not by Reason and skill, but by contingency and play. Let it be: let the world make itself. Relativity and play are highly creative, whereas "absolutes" create nothing. Absolutes are utterly useless. They are sterile.

The question next arises of how far this outlook can be viewed as a continuation of the older mystical traditions. In India we are familiar with the notion of the world as a magical show, as play, as a dance. But what of the West?

In the West, the outstanding figure at this point in the argument is Meister Eckhart.[1] Eckhart (ca.1260–1327 CE) was born some 35 years later than Aquinas, his "brother Thomas." He lived in a period when the Church and religious thought generally were coming to be dominated (as they still are) by lawyers and legalistic thinking. When the canonists have taken over, religion is seen as "creed" or "belief," and religious expressions are considered only in terms of whether the doctrines maintained in them are lawful or unlawful. Against such a background, Eckhart is the extreme case of the mystic as writer. He doesn't describe his experiences, confess his faith, or propound doctrines, and he doesn't teach a spiritual discipline; he merely plays dazzling games with language. He is so literary that John D. Caputo, in an excellent article on Eckhart's relation to deconstruction,[2] has compared him with Mallarmé and

Joyce. Such a person sees reality itself as a dance of language: as Eckhart himself puts it, "God calls himself a word . . . beside this Word, man is a byword!"[3] and later: "Every creature is full of God and is a book."[4]

In his best-known discussion of Eckhart,[5] Derrida's chief concern is to distinguish *différance* from the negative theology. *Différance* (not itself a proper word) is transcendental; it is the unthing or non-process that makes linguistic meaning possible. From a background differential matrix a meaning emerges by differentiating itself away from its Other, its antonym, and deferring it. The antonym or Other doesn't disappear. It cannot; so it is instead deferred, postponed, or made to come second. It remains hovering, excluded, in the background, because it must; it is needed to provide contrast. The dominant, ascribed meaning has to be accompanied or "haunted" by its excluded, deferred, contrasting Other – which in its turn will bring with it further associations, exclusions, and so forth, in an endless chain.

A consequence of this account is that all meaning is relative, and nothing can be described absolutely – not even God, because any word used about God will depend for its meaning upon its excluded Other, and so will have the effect of tying God back into a lengthening chain of differences and exclusions. The possibility then suggests itself that we may fit Eckhart's version of the negative theology into this account. For Eckhart, as is well known, prays to be rid of God,[6] and says that we must for God's sake take leave of God.[7] It seems that he is rejecting one account of God in order to come back and affirm God in another and "higher" way. Perhaps (it may be claimed) he is anticipating Derrida: he is insisting that we must indeed take leave of any God who is describable in human language, because the true God, the Godhead (*deitas*), is *différance*, the non-word, non-concept, non-thing prior to language that makes all meaning possible. The Negative Theology/*Différance* God would then be a universal, ineffable, transcendental condition of everything – but not itself "a being" at all.

Derrida, having raised this possibility, rejects it, saying that Eckhart and every other negative theologian is still a realistic theist. "The negative movement of the discourse on God is only a phase of positive ontotheology." Negative theology denies that God exists in the everyday sense, but only in order to prepare the way for an affirmation that God nevertheless *does* exist in some ineffable, inconceivable, higher, and purer sense. God's Being is so pure that he cannot be thought of as *a* being, among others.

So Derrida, ironically, saves Eckhart for ontotheology and for orthodoxy. He pushes Eckhart away from himself and back into the arms of "brother Thomas" and his modern Dominican defenders.

Worse: in stating his view Derrida involves himself in the very ways of thinking from which he himself (and Eckhart too) is trying to deliver us. Just like a canon-lawyer-Inquisitor, and just like a modern detector of "unsoundness," Derrida is reading Eckhart only in order to sniff out precisely what metaphysical dogma he teaches, and then consigning him to one camp or another accordingly.[8] But how can that be done, on Derrida's own view of language; and in any case, how can it be done to a text such as Eckhart's, which has surely been carefully written in such a way as to make a legalist reading of it seem obviously inappropriate and absurd?

To return Eckhart to orthodoxy is surely to misunderstand him. Orthodoxy is a legal construction. It presents a vocabulary and a complex system of rules, written and unwritten, governing what and may not be said in it. Such a system is not easily overthrown from the outside, but it can be destabilized from within, by writing that appears to accept its definitions and rules but runs in such a way as to generate paradoxes and so turn the system against itself.

Eckhart does this with such energy and exuberance that in only a few paragraphs he can and he does skip all the way from Thomas Aquinas to the mysticism of secondariness.

He very often begins from one of a small group of favourite themes. There are four of these in particular:

1 the standard metaphysical doctrine of God, as taught for example by "brother Thomas";
2 God's simplicity;

3   the human soul as made by God in the image of God, and
     as destined to become like God; and
4   purity of heart, or perfect disinterestedness.

When Eckhart is writing about purity of heart, his hidden
agenda is an attack upon the extreme ulteriorism, or long-
termism, then being introduced into the moral life by the influence of Aristotle. Means–end, or instrumental, reasoning was
making moral judgement as much a matter of one's own long-
term self-interest then as "personal finance" is today. Acts were
to be assessed in terms of their tendency to promote one's own
final salvation, an event that had been made almost unthink-
ably remote. Values were divided up between instrumental and
intrinsic values. The moral life was becoming so odiously calculative that no genuine innocence or spontaneity could ever be
achieved, or even envisaged. In a testing world, one was to
make a shrewd judgement about how to secure one's own long-
term best outcome: and that was moral thinking.

Against that background Eckhart is prepared to start from
God, and argue that as God acts without motive – God *has* no
motives – so we should act motivelessly. He will argue from the
divine simplicity that we should act wholeheartedly and not be
calculating. He will even argue that as God is gracious, so we
should act gratuitously. He produces a barrage of rational arguments against rationalism. He argues, along the same lines as
other Pure-Love writers, that it is not possible to draw closer to
God by the orthodox method of shrewd calculation of one's
own best long-term self-interest. One should love God with
one's whole heart, a kind of love in which means–end or instrumental rationality has no place at all. One should not love
God for the sake of one's own salvation, nor in any other way
except purely spontaneously and gratuitously. And the more
Eckhart presses this line of argument, the more he walks into
the mysticism of secondariness. For example:

> As God, having no motives, acts without them, so the just man
> acts without motives. As life lives on for its own sake, needing
> no reason for being, so the just man has no reason for doing
> what he does.[9]

The just person's love of God became more and more gratuitous, spontaneous, non-rational, and even objectless. Eckhart reveals the links between power, metaphysics, theological realism, and a highly calculative rationality. Attacking one of them, he attacks them all, and moves towards the purest non-realism:

> if you love God as a god, a ghost, a person, or as if he were something with a form – you must get rid of all that.
> How, then, shall I love him? Love him as he is, a not-god, not-ghost, apersonal, formless. Love him as he is the One, pure, sheer and limpid, in whom there is no duality; for we are to sink eternally from negation to negation in the One.[10]

Eckhart reaches the mysticism of secondariness when his quest for perfect purity of heart leads him to a disinterested and joyful affirmation of the gratuitous outpouring of life in the present moment. "The present Now-moment gathers up all parts of time into itself."[11] And Eckhart moves towards a straight equation of the love of (i.e. *for*) God with the love of "life," or secondariness:

> however bad life is, still there is the desire to live. Why do you eat? Why sleep? So that you may live. Why do you desire goods or honours? You know very well why. Life is so desirable in itself that one wants it for its own sake. Even those who are in the eternal pains of hell still do not want to part with their lives, whether souls or fiends, because life is so precious, flowing immediately out of God into the soul. That is why they want to live.
> What is life? God's being is my life, but if it is so, then what is God's must be mine and what is mine God's. God's is-ness (*istigkeit*) is my is-ness, and neither more nor less . . .[12]

So God is simply the Fountain (in my own terminology), the self-outpouring play of pure secondariness (or contingency, or "life") that continually produces me and my world from moment to moment. And in that self-outpouring play Eckhart insists that everything is equal – God, angel, man, woman, beast, and everything else. "Even God passes away!"[13] he says, presciently, but meaning no doubt that life itself, the Fountain, pours out and passes away all the time. It *is* its own self-giving, its own outpouring. One might even say that Christ's death only dramatizes a passing-away that is already God's, all the time. God is his own perpetual self-outpouring in the Now-moment.

Eckhart's writing moves in the same direction when he starts from Brother Thomas's metaphysical doctrine of God. God is infinite Spirit, omnipresent in his entire essence, presence and power, and always nearer to us than we are to our own selves: and God is both simple and *actus purus*, Pure Act. That means that in God there are no distinctions and no unfulfilled potentialities. God is always and absolutely the Same, everywhere and at all times, without any difference. He is unchangingly everything, everywhere, always.

To see what this means, imagine a painted portrait of God. It would of course have to be simply a plain white canvas. Perhaps it would have to be of infinite size, and perhaps multidimensional; but anyway, the main point is that it has to be simply plain brilliant white, "without any variation or shadow" as the New Testament writer puts it (*James* 1:17).

Imagine, then, a representation that is simply unbounded uniform brilliant white: is this a portrayal of absolute Being or of absolute Nothingness? Of course, one cannot say. In two senses at once, *there's no difference* – which is the point that Eckhart is making in his elaborate play with the words God, Being, and Nothingness. Language itself being just a system of differences, it cannot operate in a region where *ex hypothesi* there *is* no difference. Language only begins to engage with anything if we come forward, into the outpouring Fountain of be-ing in the present moment. Here, there is nothing *but* an outrushing play of difference, pure secondariness. *Esse est deus* is Eckhart's formula; Be-ing is God. Here, I suggest, we should (with Martin Heidegger perhaps)[14] locate Eckhart's idea of God. Be-ing, life, the outpouring play of secondariness in the Now-moment: that is as close as language, or we, can ever get to God. Eckhart is clear that be-ing's self-outpouring is its own ground (at least, in the sense that I have given to be-ing):

If anyone went on for a thousand years asking of life: "Why are you living?," life, if it could answer, would only say: "I live so that I may live." That is because life lives out of its own ground and springs from its own source, and so it lives without asking itself why it is living.[15]

Thus I am disagreeing with Derrida's derogatory interpretation of Eckhart as merely orthodox, as just another mediocre ontotheologian. I am suggesting rather that Eckhart creates a literary effect of religious happiness and spiritual liberation by the high-spirited way in which he skips from Brother Thomas to the mysticism of secondariness. Interested only in government, the Church authorities treated, and still treat, religious language as law; interested in happiness and spiritual freedom, Eckhart treats it as poetry.

An important feature of the mysticism of secondariness is that it begins to use the word "Eternity" in a new way. After the end of the old metaphysical belief in a timeless world-above, "Eternity" begins to be used in connection with a state of enraptured absorption in the presently unfolding Now-moment. Meditating with one's eyes open, one is given over to – "ecstatically immanent" in – the silently outpouring flux of be-ing. This is the postmodern spirituality: it is eternal joy in pure contingency. It is to be found in Nietzsche, of course; but something of it begins to emerge in Eckhart. And with good reason, too.

In the high Middle Ages the combination of a supernaturalist world-view, a vast historical Grand Narrative, means–end rationality, and an inordinate craving for power together produced a religious System so huge and overweening as almost to make religious happiness impossible. Where was the Good World to be found? In the remote past from which Tradition derived its authority, and again in the remotest future when, probably after hundreds of thousands of years in Purgatory, a few holy souls in each generation would be admitted to the bliss of Heaven; but never in the present. Here below one was to be content with discipline, subjection, and religious alienation. There was one consolation: one could admire the magnificent ritual and art in which the System expressed and celebrated its own vast admiration for itself.

In order to create religious happiness in his hearers, Eckhart the preacher has to find a way to concertina or telescope the whole spread-out System, bringing it all back into the present moment in life. How is he to do this? By writing his way from God's Eternal Now to the Now-moment in our human experience. There was in Boethius a classical definition of eternity as the perfect and simultaneous possession of everlasting life.[16] It was possible to say that God's Eternal "standing" Now includes all times within itself. Indeed, something of the kind had already been said by Augustine:

> Thy years neither go nor come . . . All thy years stand together as one, since they are abiding . . . thy years do not pass away . . . Thy "today" yields not to tomorrow and does not follow yesterday. Thy "today" is eternity.[17]

Boethius takes a similar line: the temporality of the created Universe is spread out successively, but in God it is all concertinaed into his non-successive standing Now.

The dominant tradition of Anselm, Aquinas, and their successors struggled to remove temporality from God altogether. But the raw statements of Augustine and Boethius give Eckhart the starting-point he needs. God's own superabundant Eternal Now totalizes all times into the divine simplicity. This is an axiom. But God is the Fountain. He perpetually pours himself out into the Now-moment of our life. So, if we give ourselves completely into the Now-moment, received as God's self-giving, we participate in his own Eternal standing Now. We experience *everything*, totalized into the Now-moment; eternal happiness in the solar efflux of pure contingency. All eternity, here and now.

It follows that we do not have to suppose that we are stuck within the limits imposed by the particular stage of the cosmic drama of redemption inside which we happen to be living. In principle, other times can also be accessed, and eternal happiness *can* be enjoyed in the Now. All we have to do is to get our own relation to existence right. Just get on to the leading edge of the Now-moment and wait very still and attentive, until you find yourself beginning to surf it.

Eckhart describes the surfing thus: in it

> Action and becoming are one. If the carpenter does no work, the
> house is not built. When his broadaxe stops, construction stops.
> God and I are one in process. He acts and I become . . .[18]

Eckhart even says that since to live in the *Nu*, the Now-
moment, is to participate in God's eternity, someone who lived
thus all the time would never grow old:

> For the Now-moment in which God made the first man, and the
> Now-moment in which I am speaking are all one in God, in
> whom there is only one Now. Look! The person who lives in the
> light of God is conscious neither of time past nor of time to come
> but only of the one eternity.[19]

Eckhart has one more hint as to what he means by living in
the *Nu*, the Now-moment. He says that we should let go of our
own ideas; we should be free and empty of them.[20] So the trick
is unreservedly to abandon oneself to the outpouring of pure
secondariness in the Now, until one feels oneself upborne by it.
That's eternity in the moment, that is the Eternal Generation of
the Son in oneself, that is supreme happiness. Surfing Now.

Eckhart is preaching popular sermons in the German vernacular. By not using Latin, he gives himself more freedom of
thought. Clever of him. He makes language dance, but he is not
pretending to formulate a rigorous argument. Nor is he in any
way a describer of an extraordinary way of knowing supernatural religious facts. Eckhart is not a "mystic" in the popular
sense that I have called "Modern." Rather, Eckhart has found
a way of writing religious happiness. Starting from incontest-
ably orthodox premises, he skips his way to the mysticism of
secondariness, and in so doing he radically destabilizes the System and makes it tremble. No wonder he was brought to trial
at Cologne in 1326, and then posthumously censured by Pope
John XXII in 1329. What he was doing was something very like
deconstruction, and very like the radical theology of the past
two centuries. He lived (as we still live) in a period when the

religious System was old, overgrown, deeply unhappy, alienating and alienated. He sought to write his way and ours out
of its tyranny and into religious happiness. In the process he
became perhaps the very first Western teacher of the mysticism
of secondariness.

*   *   *   *

Eckhart can sound very like a modern radical theologian. He
tries to bring down all the metaphysics, and also to telescope
together the spread-out Grand Narrative theology of religion, so
as to produce an effect of burning joy and intensity in the *Nu*,
the Now-moment. In the fully developed doctrine-system of the
Church, the living substance of religion has all been projected
out, rationalized, and turned into a great cosmic ideology, which
has served as the world-view of an entire civilization. When
that ideology becomes oppressive, the mystical writer seeks to
reverse the process and telescope it all back down again into the
Now, into the heart, into the Fountain, into a felt relation to the
outpouring flux of existence.

The radical theologian's purpose is much the same as the
mystic's. Since the Enlightenment we have burst out of the old
religious cosmology and grand-narrative history. They now seem
absurdly primitive. Now that we have our physical cosmology,
we no longer need the old sacred cosmology; and now that we
have our modern critical history, we no longer need the old
sacred history of the world. So the radical theologian attempts
to "de-objectivize" or "demythologize" the spread-out religious
System, telescoping it all back down into the felt relation to the
forthcoming of life in the Now. And Ludwig Feuerbach is an
excellent example of a Lutheran "radical theologian" who carries out such a programme in the full knowledge that he is
following in the footsteps not just of Luther but also of a line
of late-medieval mystics:

> Reason is the truth of Nature, the heart is the truth of man. To
> speak popularly, reason is the God of Nature, the heart the God
> of man . . . Everything which man wishes, but which reason,
> which Nature denies, the heart bestows. God, immortality, free-
> dom, in the supernaturalistic sense, exist only in the heart. The

heart is itself the existence of God, the existence of immortality. Satisfy yourself with this existence! You do not understand your heart; therein lies the evil. You desire a real, external, objective immortality, a God out of yourselves. Here is the source of delusion.

The Essence of Christianity (1841) Appendix,
Sect. 2 (George Eliot translation)

CHAPTER EIGHT

meltdown

The subject of mysticism is perhaps returning to the Western agenda: at any rate, two ambitious works have recently come from Chicago.[1] Each deals only with Western Christian mysticism, and each is the first instalment of a projected multivolume work. Bernard McGinn's *The Foundations of Mysticism: origins to the fifth century* is a very substantial piece of traditional-style historical theology, and in my terms is Modern in outlook. Michel de Certeau's *La Fable mystique: XVIe–XVIIe siècle* appeared in French in 1982. The author died in 1986 and this, the only volume of his work to be seen through the press by him personally, appeared in an English translation in 1992. De Certeau, though a Jesuit priest, was a member of the brilliant group of intellectuals who attended Jacques Lacan's seminars, and is (or at least, ought to be) postmodern in outlook.

There might be two reasons why Christian mysticism should be thought important today. Some will say, it is because mystical theology is experiential theology, or "spiritual" theology, and closely linked with Christian ethics. McGinn might favour a reply along such lines. Others though might say that mystical theology is interesting because it is an "alternative" or "minoritarian" tradition, rebellious, deconstructive, and unpopular because it has always worked against the traditional dogmatic theology, which was constructed as an ideological justification for the power and authority of the Church hierarchy. The Christian tradition (and the Muslim, and others, too) is not monolithic. It does not speak with one voice. It always had its own internal Other, an *anti-tradition* of radical dissent. As we have already argued, if the mystics were such a saintly and orthodox lot, why were they persecuted? And if their distinguishing characteristics have to do with their way of experiencing "the Presence of God" (to quote McGinn's main title), why is it that they turn out uniformly to be *writers*, who were punished not for having heretical experiences but for publishing heretical doctrines?

In his book, de Certeau limits himself to Catholic Western Europe in the period between the Renaissance and the Enlightenment. The mystics were typically people neither heavily involved in the old ecclesiastical power-structure, like Bossuet, nor a part of the newly emerging dominant culture of the State, the professions and the intellectuals, like Descartes. The mystics were relatively marginal people in a culture undergoing profound change, who therefore, says de Certeau, experienced their relationship with God as "absence." They devised new and often fanciful systems of thought and experimented with language in their attempts to reach out to a God who had been steadily slipping away since the breakup of the great medieval synthesis. And de Certeau moves some way towards our own view by recognizing that, at least since the seventeenth century, mysticism has been primarily a literary phenomenon.

Despite his title, de Certeau evidently traces the pedigree of the kind of mysticism that interests him back to the Middle Ages. In Carolingian and Romanesque times just about everyone was closely bound into the military aristocracy, or the peasantry, or the Church. Town life was at a low ebb. But gradually in northern France, in the Netherlands, and along the Rhine valley the towns grew and prospered. In them typically urban patterns of religious life reappeared for the first time since Antiquity. Urban religion is usually more informal and volatile. Women, and lay people generally, are prominent. People enjoy public parades, voluntary associations, good works, and personal devotion. Large numbers of small informal religious communities spring up – and some of them attract unfavourable attention.

Such was the environment in which fourteenth-century mysticism flourished, and one might say that for de Certeau the whole period 1300–1700, from Eckhart to Molinos and Madame Guyon, is dominated by the slow painful transition from the medieval to the modern world, the fraying and fading of "the sacred canopy," and the withdrawal of God. Throughout this period the mystics tried to elaborate a complex language of spirituality. They pictured the spiritual life of the individual as a long journey through many stages, and they portrayed the inner world of the soul as a Garden of Delights, an Interior Castle, and a great Palace. What was being lost as objective cultural fact might thus be regained by enriching the world of subjectivity. The mystics, one might say, were trying to write the emergence of the Modern type of urban religious consciousness.

This suggests a certain proportionality: the mystics were in the same sort of position relative to the culture of their time as the various New Age and other counter-cultural movements are in relation to the violent upheavals of our own time. The tone of voice in which Bossuet ridicules "mysticism" (then a newly coined and derisive term) is the same as the tone of voice in which a leading scientist of today will ridicule popular "superstition." Indeed, Establishment figures like Bossuet were so successful in giving the mystics a bad name that, says de Certeau, the very word was still not in the dictionary in the eighteenth century, "and would not appear in the title of a published work until the nineteenth century."[2] The fact that the mystics, after having lain sunk in such ill-repute for so long, were suddenly rehabilitated and promoted so high by their former critics shows how desperate for support the orthodox had become by the nineteenth century.

My account has, however, differed considerably from that of de Certeau. I have suggested that from the first there was conflict in Christianity between two main strands, one priestly and institutional, the other prophetic and charismatic. The priestly tradition sees the Church as Catholic and Apostolic, an unchanging, disciplined, and cohesive institution in which Law, Truth and the means of Grace are controlled entirely by the successors of the Apostles. By the Middle Ages the "spirituality," the whole body of professional ecclesiastical persons, was a very large and dominant Church within the Church and a semi-independent Estate of the Realm, a hugely powerful and privileged system of religious mediation which deferred not merely till after death, but until several hundred thousands of years after death, the actual delivery of the salvation it promised. Worship (or, at least, ceremonial) was this mighty System's symbolic self-celebration. It took place indeed in a distinct world, the sacred world, where "the religious" lived. The laity watched worship from the profane world on the other side of a screen, just as in today's society "the masses" are still watching "the stars" performing on the other side of a screen.

In the second and third centuries the clergy had been successful in seizing total control of the Church. Those they defeated were branded as heretics – Montanists, Gnostics, and suchlike. People in this subordinated "prophetic" tradition value personal experience and charismatic, rather than institutionally accredited, leadership. They are not particularly historically minded, and they tend to be urban and short-termist in outlook.

In her sympathetic book on *The Gnostic Gospels*,[3] Elaine Pagels has emphasized the historic importance of the early victory of the male priesthood and the principle of patriarchy in the Church. But the other tradition, though suppressed, never quite died. It has lingered on as a literary tradition of protest against mediated and institutional religion.

De Certeau sees in the mystics of his chosen period a certain "mourning" for the death or withdrawal of God, and "nostalgia"[4] – his word again – for the lost unities of the Middle Ages. But if the mystics were really romantic conservatives looking back nostalgically to the Middle Ages, why did the religious authorities persecute them so fiercely? I suggest that the mystics stand rather in an older tradition of religious radicalism that goes back to Jesus and to the prophets before him, and has always objected to mediated religion and the indefinite deferral of salvation in a system that profits from the delay. Urban people – as we see in our own day – are not too thrilled by promises of post-mortem compensation for present hardships. They want it now. Why not? So mystical writing always attempts to deconstruct those orthodox doctrines (about God and the soul, etc.) that stand in the way of religious happiness; and mystical writing also seeks to find ways of bypassing the officially controlled channels of salvation. It is not content with an indefinitely long wait in detention. It passionately yearns for religious happiness, and as soon as may be.

Mystical writing, I have suggested, always seeks to circumvent or to deconstruct the great distinctions by means of which the professionally religious, the élite Church within the Church, have historically sought to secure their own status and have postponed salvation. Large tracts of what is usually thought of as "theology" therefore make little appearance in mystical writing. One notices the absence of the familiar historical narratives of legitimation that include accounts of revelation, of the Fall, Original Sin, and Redemption, of the significance of the Church, the ministry, and the sacraments, of promise and fulfilment, and of authority and tradition. Such matters are little mentioned: but what *is* prominent in mystical writing is the relation between the individual human soul and God. Here orthodoxy seems very cold in its insistence that even in a state of beatitude the Creator/creature distinction remains, and the soul and God are numerically still two and not one. I am finite: if God remains an Other, distinct from me and an actual Infinite Reality, then the disproportion between us is infinite, and my state of exile or alienation is oddly unthinkable. For where is there for me to *be*, outside of or distinct from the Infinite?

Here one sees why the analogy of sexual union has been considered so acceptable by the orthodox, because in sexual union the parties remain numerically two even while they are as closely united as the heart could desire. To which, as we saw earlier, some Spanish theorists replied that sexual love is haunted by anguish precisely because it never achieves and cannot achieve the *complete* Enosis or one-ing that it longs for.[5] If we are to find *complete* happiness in religion, it must eventually deliver more than sexual love ever can.

Accordingly mystical writing, both in the "Abrahamic" and in the "Indian" traditions, everywhere tends towards non-dualism. In the non-dualist sort of experience there is no distinction either between the subject and the field of experience, or within the field of experience. So at least it is said; and the attractiveness of non-dualism is such that even those like John of the Cross, who use the sexual analogy with the most boldness, still try to push it a step further by saying, for example, that the Mistress is "transformed into" her Lover.[6]

The issues here are not easy, because of the striking lack of agreed and authoritative formal statements of what it is that in the religions God is supposed to be, and the soul is supposed to be, and what it may be to see and to know God in the state of beatitude. But there is one way to find out how close one can get to God without actually becoming God, and that is to take the official doctrine about the dual nature of Christ which was defined by a Council of the universal Church at Chalcedon in the year 451. Therewith we take the ideas about God and about the soul which that dogmatic definition incorporates, and also the papal statement, "The Tome of Leo," which the Council endorsed. Then in these two very highly authoritative statements we have about as clear an official account as we are likely to find of what is meant by God and by a human nature, and in what way they can be thought of as having been united while yet remaining distinct. The Incarnate Lord Jesus Christ is surely a complete human being, body and soul, who is as perfect and as completely united with God as any human being can hope to be, here or hereafter. He is, says Pope Leo, "true God in the entire and perfect nature of true man, complete in his own properties, complete in ours."[7] In him, says the Council, are two natures, divine and human, united "without confusion, without change, without division, without separation; the distinction of natures being in no way annulled by the union . . ."[8]

So Jesus the man is held to be as closely conjoined with God as it is possible to be, and no soul in Heaven can be closer. But he still needs faith. He needs to pray, and he suffers temptation. He experiences psychic storms of anger, grief and pain. So although he is at all times as close to God as it is possible for a human being to be, he seems to be no better off for it than anyone else. This appears to show that orthodox doctrine makes perfect religious happiness eternally unattainable. The divine and human natures are metaphysically *conjoined* seamlessly, but they are not actually fused or confused. They remain distinct, so clearly distinct that the man Jesus in his human nature still seems to know God only by faith and to be, despite his extraordinary human gifts, just as vulnerable to ignorance, temptation, and suffering as the rest of us. So if this is so in the uniquely close case of the Incarnation, what can union with God be for the rest of us?

It may be commented here that in the orthodox doctrine of Christ the two complete natures, divine and human, are not only *conjoined* metaphysically, but in addition are *united* in the

"Person" of the eternal Word; which makes the case of Christ somewhat different from the case of anyone who follows him. True: but I reply that this consideration only strengthens my argument, by making it into an *a fortiori* argument. If being quite exceptionally united with God, in the way he was, still made so little apparent difference even to Jesus (who in the Gospels appears simply as one suffering human being among others), how much good can it do to *us*?

An alternative view of Christ, put forward in those days by Theodore of Mopsuestia and Nestorius, says that the union in Christ of a man with God was a *moral* union; and Theodore expressly compares it with the union of husband and wife.[9] This is revealing, because it brings out the close connection between the Christian doctrine about Christ and mystical ideas about the Spiritual Marriage and union with God. For now the mystic in passive contemplation, the soul in Heaven, and Jesus on Earth are all of them in *exactly* the same position. They are all in perfect moral union with God. As before, the same question arises: to all appearances, Jesus doesn't seem to be any better off than anyone else. He doesn't have any special knowledge, or special happiness, or special protection against evil and suffering. In fact he has a terrible time. So again, Christianity (along with the other monotheistic faiths) is stuck with ideas about God, about "Man," and about the impossibility of their fusion into numerical unity, which have the effect of making complete religious happiness an eternal impossibility. It seems that nothing short of the full deification of our humanity will do; but that we can't have, and not even the man Jesus got it.

It has often been said that "Chalcedon was trying to square the circle"; that because the Council was working with philosophical ideas about "God" and "Man" that defined them as opposites, it was bound to be unable to give a coherent account of their union in Christ. But the situation is much more dramatic than that: the position is that all classical monotheism makes it impossible to understand how a finite human mind (that thinks through categories) can know God (who transcends them all), how it is possible to love God, and how a finite spiritual substance, the human self, can find complete happiness in being united with the infinite God without being permitted the blissful engulfment that it naturally longs for. And what sort of sense does it make *anyway* to say that the Infinite and a finite being are and must remain numerically two, side by side? (Can the *mathematical* infinite and a unit be numerically two, side by side?)

It is objected at this point that I am quite wrong to model the relation between Infinite and finite beings on the relation between infinite and finite qualities. I should rather be guided by Kierkegaard's phrase "the infinite qualitative difference," and should see the Infinite as a qualitatively different order, or mode, of being. In which case the Infinite and I may coexist, independent of each other and without colliding.

Very well: but a move of this type, by making God the Wholly Other, only makes matters worse. God becomes absolutely or metaphysically unknowable and hidden from us, an idea that cannot even be stated without intolerable paradox, and that creates an effect of truly dreadful religious despair and frustration.

It should be apparent by now that the victory of fully developed philosophical monotheism in the Church, the conquest of the Church by "the successors of the Apostles," God's becoming infinite and unknowable, and Christianity's becoming a sacramentally mediated religion in which final religious happiness is so problematic that it is deferred until long, long after death – these four events were all of them so many different aspects of the same event, which took place, perhaps, in the third and fourth centuries. The bishops took charge, saying: "You can't have God, for the present at least; but here are we, your Fathers in God, and this is the Faith that you are to believe."

There was from the first an obvious objection to the orthodoxy that developed. Once God had become actual infinite Spirit, simple, omnipresent, and all-powerful, he was *already* everything, everywhere and always, but in a way that transcends our understanding and escapes our language. So God is unknowable, and we must accept that we can be allowed no more than the elaborate apparatus of ritual, symbolism, and belief upon authority to live by – at least in this life. *But in that case how can things be any different for us after death?* Orthodoxy says *both* that we must submit to the authority of the System in this life for the sake of eternal happiness after death *and* that after death we remain our finite selves and God remains God, so that the epistemological situation must remain unchanged. So we are assured *both* that things will become radically better after death, *and* that they cannot do so. This is a contradiction – the contradiction that the entire tradition of mystical and radical theology has struggled to overcome.[10]

The mystic's task then is to overcome the contradictions of orthodoxy and create religious happiness. This is a task for a writer. You can't first *experience* religious happiness and *then* transcribe it into words, because writing precedes experience, writing forms and produces experience, writing makes experience possible. Only when I have managed to *write* religious happiness will I "know what it is" sufficiently to be able to recognize it in experience.

What must be the mystical writer's strategy for writing her or his way into religious happiness? The task presents itself as that of deconstructing or undermining the violent ontological disjunction that separates God from the self. There are four main routes.

Internalizing God within the Self

An old, familiar phrase in Plato's *Republic* declares that the Good is above or beyond Being. In the long tradition of the Negative Theology there was always a possibility of promoting God not into total obscurity, and not merely into a higher level of "reality," but into pure ideality, so that God becomes a guiding spiritual ideal internal to the self. There has been much dispute about whether in the end we should see Meister Eckhart, or Kant, or Kierkegaard as having consciously taken this route; but it certainly *was* taken quite explicitly in a rather late mystical work called *Taking Leave of God* (1980).

Perhaps the main objection to this route is one that may be made to Kant himself: to internalize God as a regulative ideal and to internalize the legislative power and authority of moral reason in the way that Kant has done gives rise to a very grand heroic religious humanism, magnificent in its day (around 1750–1860), but now no longer a live option. As a proposed solution to the problem of religious happiness, *Taking Leave of God* asks too much of the self, makes the self too big, lays too great a burden upon the self. Even its author no longer wants to be and is no longer able to be the person the book asks him to be.

Dissolving the Self into God

Since we must all die anyway, and since we all greatly enjoy the dissolution of the self as we yield ourselves up to sleep, or sex, or visual or musical pleasure, the way of dissolving or drowning the self into God has great and obvious attractions.

It is also the way required by theology. Since God is *already* pure Act, infinite in his being, power, wisdom, and goodness, and already everything everywhere, it is an offence to reason, and it must be a form of illusion, that there should be or seem to be anything at all other than God. If the philosophers and the theologians of the past ever took their own idea of God seriously, they must have felt that the very existence of the creature is *de trop*, horrible, superfluous, unthinkable. There's a thought: the point is that it isn't *God* that is unthinkable, but *the creature*. It's not needed, there's no room for it, and it ought not to be – and that no doubt is why our most intense moments of happiness and pleasure are also moments when we feel we are swooning, fainting, dying.

The feeling that we yearn to give up our separate existence and return into the immanence or nothingness out of which we came is very deep and very strong in us all. One day you will learn that there is in you an intense thirst for death. And, contrary to what some people suppose, it is a happy feeling – so happy that we actively seek out and fall in love with those people, things, and places that arouse it in us most strongly. It has been interpreted very variously by Kierkegaard, Freud, Tillich, and Bataille. But I suspect that behind all these interpretations lies a corollary of theism that we are still most reluctant to admit: if there really is God, our existence makes no sense. We should not be. Our extinguishment will be a gain, a blessing, the removal of an ugly anomaly.

If my interpretation of it is correct, then this particular line of mystical writing will be most interesting and most actively pursued in periods when people are wrestling most actively with the questions of love, death, and God. Perhaps we should see it therefore as interwoven with Romanticism and the late-Modern period, and think of someone like Emily Brontë.[11]

The Spiritual Marriage

As we will now see, the metaphor of sexual union has all sorts of advantages. It is psychologically seductive, joining flesh and spirit, and bringing all sorts of agreeable sexual feelings into play in the religious sphere. In sex we move from initial feelings of doubt, strangeness, unease, and fear to a joyful and happy climax, so that writing sexual union is a good way of writing oneself out of religious estrangement and dread, and into religious happiness and fulfilment.

The metaphor of the Spiritual Marriage is also good for "personalism" in the religious traditions, and good for women insofar as the human who becomes the lover of a god is always seen as female in Greek mythology, in Apuleius, in Plotinus, in India, in the romance of Yahweh and Israel in the Hebrew Bible, in Christianity, and even in Islam. Male Islamic mystics are usually very cautious about casting themselves as the mistresses of God, but Ibn'l Farid (1182–1235 CE) is conspicuously bold and plays extravagant games with his gender pronouns.[12]

Sexual mysticism is tolerated, no doubt because it is *prima facie* good for orthodoxy. Both God and the soul are retained, without either of them completely engulfing the other. The picture of the soul as the object of God's desire interestingly counteracts the contrary view which I have expressed, that if the God of metaphysical theism really does exist then he cannot possibly leave any room for us to exist beside him. Our existence is an absurdity, even an impossibility, and we ought to get rid of ourselves. To overcome our doubts here, sexual mysticism may use (as Kierkegaard does) the old parable of King Cophetua and the beggarmaid, a story of which there are variants in many traditions.

The main objection to writing sexual mysticism is that, although it certainly makes us feel good, it does not solve the intellectual problem of how a finite being like you or me can have dealings with and be happy with the Infinite. Sexual mysticism merely rewrites God as finite. Furthermore, in the long run it has had the effect of rewriting not religion as sex, but sex as religion. Today people's sexuality has become their religion, for sex is the sphere of life in which people seek out their own true identity, and profess it publicly as their faith by "coming out." It is in the sphere of sex that people today most actively pursue personal happiness and personal growth. Very well: but in that case the religious problem still remains. Sexual happiness remains touched by anxiety. It can be lost: it will be, for death will part all lovers.

*   *   *   *

We have found some reason for dissatisfaction with each of the three lines of mystical writing so far considered. The problem was the seemingly unbridgeable metaphysical gulf between the human self and its own longed-for happiness in God. The infinity of God's being and attributes makes God incomprehensible, unknowable, and even impossible to love; and it makes the self seem to itself an absurdity. In reply, we saw that the mystical writer might attempt to promote God all the way into ideality and then relocate him in the human heart. At the opposite pole, the self might be liberated from its own absurdity by being drowned into God and so disappearing. And thirdly, one might rewrite the relation of God and the soul as a new version of the very ancient Hieros Gamos, the Sacred Marriage in the old fertility religions. This is highly appealing, and may have the agreeable effect of raising the standing of all things fertile and female; but it doesn't fully solve the religious problem. For that, we must go a step further. We don't just empty the metaphysics out of God, we don't just empty the metaphysics out of the self, and we don't try to marry the two: we empty both out completely, into each other and into universal secondariness. A double wedding and a double death.

The Double Meltdown

The most powerful kind of mystical writing is highly literary, and it cunningly exploits the space between two distinct vocabularies. One vocabulary is the mythological and poetical language of the scriptures, of worship and preaching and popular belief. The other vocabulary is much more closely defined and shows the influences of philosophy and of lawyers. It is the official "high" language in which the limits of permissible belief and practice are laid down, orthodoxy is defined, and the faith is systematized.

The crucial point is that, in order to preserve the unity of the whole religious system, it has to be claimed that the two languages are fully consistent both internally and with each other. Thus, Christians believe that the formal philosophy-influenced dogmas about God and Christ are actually "taught in scripture." They have also believed that scripture itself is or contains an internally coherent system of thought, "biblical theology." So strong is the influence of this idea that people often quite fail to notice how wildly inconsistent scripture is.

Consider, for example, "scriptural teaching" about God. Scripture solemnly assures us both that "No man has ever seen God" (I *John* 4:12, RSV) *and* that lots of men from Adam to Isaiah have seen and conversed with God; both that God, being God, of course does not repent *and*, only a few verses later, that God did repent having made Saul king over Israel (I *Samuel* 15:29, 35); both that God is vehemently opposed to there being any earthly king of Israel (I *Samuel* 8:7) *and* that he will establish the dynasty of David for ever (II *Samuel* 7).

Equally bizarre – though very seldom remarked upon – are the astonishing contradictions in the reported teaching of Jesus. For example, the Sermon of the Mount instructs us *both* to practice our religion "before men" and as publicly as possible, *and* to do the opposite (*Matthew* 5:14–16; 6:1–6). A parable in which we are told that our response to the divine invitation must be wholehearted and very prompt, without any making of excuses, is immediately followed by a saying to the effect that it's only sensible first to sit down carefully and count the cost (*Luke* 14:16–21; contrast vv. 28–32; and then another reversal of policy in v. 33).

If scripture is internally very often inconsistent, there is if anything an ever wider gap between the sober and abstract language of official doctrine, in which for example God is without body, parts, or passions, and the highly mythological and populist language of the Bible in which God has only too much of all three. But authority has to claim that both languages are co-equally authoritative, and fully consistent with each other.

Now, in order to build up any great and unified system of political or religious power, it is necessary to have control of language, control of exegesis, and systematic coherence. In order to establish the power-pyramid, there have to be orderly gradations of being, authority, rank and value. To grade and scale everything, we need to be taught everywhere to distinguish between the ultimate and the subultimate, the end and the means, the primary and the secondary, the intrinsic and the instrumental, the absolute and the relative, the remote and the proximate, and the higher and the lower generally. These distinctions being habitually made, the scales are established, and all of them are found to lead back to the Original, most holy and necessary One who is the First Cause, the ultimate explanation, the Supreme Good and the *raison d'être* of everything.

Thus it is by the use of power to control language that great metaphysical truths and realities are established within language, and in particular the monarchy of reason in the soul, of the king or *pontifex* on Earth, and of God in Heaven. Everything depends upon the use of social power to control language and interpretation. You have to believe – and the people do believe – that the Holy Book and the holy and orthodox Faith make up a complete and systematically coherent whole which must be maintained intact and may not be tampered with. Over-daring, playful, or mischievous exegesis is very dangerous because it makes people feel that the entire House they inhabit has begun to shake and tremble.

Nevertheless, that is what the kind of mystic I am now describing does. This writer moves about in the wide spaces created, both by the gap between the formal language of doctrine and the poetical language of scripture, and by the severe internal inconsistencies within scripture itself. Because mystical writing is so highly political – one is, after all, using language mockingly in order to subvert absolute power, an extremely dangerous game – it is necessary to cover one's tracks, and there are a variety of standard ways of doing this. One writes poetry, professedly follows distinguished precedent, adopts the anthropomorphic vocabulary of scripture, and preaches in the vernacular to ordinary people. One uses complex allegories – and all this is done with the aim of maintaining plausible deniability.

Just because the tradition is so complex, and the language of scripture in particular is so riotously anthropomorphic and inconsistent, a skilled and witty performer like Eckhart is very good at maintaining deniability, as one sees in his point-by-point written *Defence* in response to minute and detailed charges of heresy.[13]

I am saying here that the reason why mystics use language in the strange ways they do is twofold: on the one hand, they are trying to play games with language in such a way as to destabilize structures of religious oppression that are firmly built into language.[14] They are trying to recreate religious freedom and a spirit of levity, within a tradition that has become a cruel and alienating power-structure. But, on the other hand, they are acutely conscious of being surrounded by enemies who will seize upon a careless word and use it to destroy them. In this respect, they are like Jesus being questioned by his enemies, like a suspect comedian or writer under communist government or in Islam, like a modern politician being questioned by a journalist, or like a liberal lecturer in a fundamentalist-controlled seminary. They have to watch their words. If a mystic's writing sometimes appears far-fetched or fanciful, the reason is not that he or she is a soulful eccentric with idiosyncratic ideas about heavenly matters, but rather that religious utterance is surrounded by very severe pressures and threats of a political kind.

Mystical writing was indeed the forerunner of today's radical theology and deconstruction; and our analysis helps to explain how it is that Jacques Derrida can be described *both* as an intellectual subversive whose work leads to the view that any text may be interpreted to mean almost anything, *and* as a mystic. Well, yes, mystical writing is indeed politically and linguistically subversive and always was so. It has to be. Our religious vocabulary was long ago seized by power and tied to certain extremely alienating metaphysical ideas. Much though we love it, our religion is rightly politicized and oppressive. The mystic seeks to create an effect of religious happiness by liberating religious language from the Babylonian captivity of metaphysics. When the writing does succeed in melting God and the soul down into each other, the effect of happiness is astonishing.

The meltdown reduces God, the self, and everything to secondariness: fluid, living, foundationless, and unbounded secondariness, in which we are engulfed and lost.

Eckhart himself, as we have seen, most often reaches this effect by starting from the impeccably orthodox-sounding theme of purity of heart. We must be perfect as God is perfect. We must love God with all our heart and mind and soul and strength. We must love God with a pure heart, in utter singleness of will and without any ulterior motive or admixture of motives. We must be fully disinterested in our love of God. Our love for God must be fully pure, motiveless, disinterested, even gratuitous. And now, when Eckhart has talked away any thought of antecedent hidden motives or further aims, we suddenly realize that he's made the purest religious feeling into a matter of just *play*! Non-rational, gratuitous, spontaneous play. Starting with the irreproachably orthodox theme of purity of heart, Eckhart has developed a covert attack on the instrumental rationality that builds metaphysics and harnesses life in the service of power. Eckhart's aim is in the end to give us religious joy in the play of pure secondariness. Happiness is gratuitousness, folly.

We live in a culture in which too many people still think like slaves. They think that a human life not dominated by metaphysics and lived in the service of power is "meaningless." They want to be told what to do. That is why they attack deconstruction as being nihilistic, and as asserting universal meaninglessness; and that is why they fear the attack on dogmatic realism in religion. It threatens to end the state of subjection which they call having a sense of purpose in one's life, and which they identify with reason and true religion. They passionately love their own state of enslavement: they have built an elaborate ideology around it, and they will not quickly be persuaded to give it up.

The task of the religious writer now is to find a way of writing the mysticism of secondariness sufficiently seductive to detach people from their old dead gods.

CHAPTER NINE

happiness

By religious happiness (or eternal happiness, or salvation) I mean a happiness that so fills a person and her world that she can be confident that it will never entirely forsake her, however bad things get to be. It can and it does remain with one even during very severe suffering, which makes it the sort of happiness that delivers us from the fear of death; with it, as the saying goes, one can "die happy." Like a great love, this sort of happiness colours everything. But since everything is relative, it too is relative, and I should add that I find (and, I suspect, everybody finds) that we become aware of this cosmic or world-filling sort of happiness chiefly by contrast with certain other things from which we find it has delivered us. Thus the "mysticism of secondariness" is to be given over to and made completely happy by a certain vision of life and of the world; and it makes me happy because it has freed me from certain threats, fears, and oppressive feelings. No doubt it was always the case that the feeling of having been saved or redeemed first presented itself as a feeling of ease or relief at having been delivered from something that was grating uncomfortably all the time.

I say this, by way of an acknowledgement that the mysticism of secondariness makes one happy just because it is a reversal of and a deliverance from an older vision of the world that has for generations been becoming less and less comfortable. In fact, I am going to suggest that the classical "realistic" idea of God has become very uncomfortable indeed, being associated with a picture of the human condition and of human nature that now seems ferociously and unbearably pessimistic. We really do need to be freed from it, and mystical writing indicates how this liberation might come about.

An indication that we are indeed moving away from the classical idea of God is given by the fact that nowadays God is spoken of chiefly as Love, and chiefly in cosmological terms.

People say that to believe in God is to believe that deep down the Universe is not a howling indifferent chaos, but is friendly to human beings and their values. So people say; but this is a very recent line of talk that has developed only in the past half-century or so. In the older prayer books of the Reformation and of the Latin and Greek churches, God is addressed first and principally as Almighty and Everlasting, as a King, Lord, and Judge. The Jews similarly address God first as King of the Universe, and the Muslims simply call God "Great." So far as we human beings are concerned, the attributes of God that matter most and come first are his unlimited power over us and his sovereign freedom from the limitations of space and time. Unlike us, he never gets old and he never sleeps, so there is no escape from him.

The Almighty

God's power and might was originally and primarily political and cultural. We should set aside the Cosmos for the present, because the first world we ever recognized was the world of language, a world of symbolic exchange, a cultural world, a *society*. The ancient Jews saw their God as the one who had called Israel into being long before they saw God as the one who had called the Cosmos into being, and they were right.[1] The social world, the world of meaning, the world of language precedes the natural world and is much larger and more complex. The world of meaning is what we live in all the time. It's the air we breathe. As for "the Universe," it plays little part in our lives. Have you ever known it to *bear upon* you, or to make a difference in your life? Of course you haven't; our worlds are very diverse and fragmented, and we see little to justify the way the word "Universe" seems to bind everything up into a coherent totality. Perhaps the world could never have been perceived as a unified Cosmos, until people had first learnt the discipline of religious and political monarchy.

Human beings are very difficult and disorderly creatures. The development first of clans and tribes, and then of the earliest law-governed State societies, required a huge exertion of disciplinary power. Early speech-acts were predominantly imperatives, sharp commands. We moderns have in the past two or three generations suddenly become very soft and easygoing, and it is easy to forget how savagely harsh life was for nearly everyone until quite recently, and how terrifying social authority had to be, and was. That is why every human being is troubled in ways that no animal is (apart, of course, from animals kept in captivity by us), for it was pitiless severity and not love that first created us, shaped our psychology, made us human, made us the way we are; and to this day most people accept without question the fact that human life is lived, and has to be lived, in a state of subjection to unconditional power and authority. Only occasionally does something happen that brings home to us all what this can still mean.

An illustration from the present century comes from the trenches of the First World War. Millions of young men suddenly found themselves drafted into military service, given a uniform, a rifle, and a few weeks training, and then sent out to the Front. There they dug trenches and waited until they were ordered to go over the top and walk into a hail of machine-gun fire. They did it, dying in millions. Why? Because what was behind them, the authority of the State, was very much greater and more terrifying than what was before them. A court martial, a last night of waiting, and a dishonourable death by firing squad was a much more fearsome prospect than obeying orders, and dying a quick and honourable death on the field of battle. You loved your country so much as to give your life for it, because it frightened you much more than the enemy did. It was not the enemy, but your own side that had the real power over you.

The general principle which this illustration reminds us of is that in order to turn a wayward animal into a disciplined and socialized human being there had to be enforced common subjection to a unifying principle of unconditional power and authority of which people are more afraid even than they are of death itself. It is striking that Jesus himself reportedly stresses that God's power is much more dreadful than the power of an earthly absolute monarch. God searches the heart, his punishment is inescapable, and there can be no hope of a blessed release in death (*Matthew* 10:28; compare 5:22, 30; *Hebrews* 10:26–31). In short, those people who really did "believe in God" in the sense that was standard until the Enlightenment, and even until the mid-nineteenth century, believed themselves to be living under a system of totalitarian government that was infinitely greater and more crushing than the one imagined by George Orwell. That was *their* normality: they lived with it always.

How were people able to bear such terrorism? It was universal; it became part of our psychology. We are very profoundly accustomed to it. The themes of the Judgement of the Dead and the torment of the damned seem to be the single most widespread religious beliefs, and topics of religious art, all around the world.[2] They are found in every civilization from Ancient Egypt onwards, with the possible exception of the civilizations of pre-Columbian America, whose beliefs are still not yet well understood. In the Old World the Christian dates are typical: the Doom-painting continues until the sixteenth century,[3] and the Hellfire sermon until as late as the early twentieth century. Even today we still hear people say: "I hope he rots in Hell," which means that they think it a very desirable state of affairs that every human being should be consciously subject to the Judgement of an absolute Power that will in the end dispose of each one of us as it sees fit. That which has absolute power must know everything and must in the end fix everything, judge everyone, and audit all accounts. His Judgement is absolute, and there is no appeal.

In many of the great religions the theme of absolute power is overlaid and veiled by a reassurance to the effect that God is the Merciful, the Compassionate; God is faithful, righteous, and loving. But the underlying nightmare is still present. The fear of God: some people think it still needs to be there to keep us human. Without it, we would run wild.

You may ask: Why do we so passionately yearn for God and love God, if God frightens the wits out of us? But there is no paradox here. The notion of absolute subjection to something that is unconditionally sovereign over us links religion and politics. The young rifleman walking into machine-gun fire in the First World War is giving his life for the love of his country because it is human nature to fall violently in love with that which has absolute power over you and terrifies you beyond measure. A kinky lot, we eroticize the thing that fills us with horror, in order to make it bearable. People taken hostage by armed hijackers begin to identify with their captors. Indeed, we actively seek out a state of subjection: we will vote in the largest numbers for the strongest leader. We want to be ruled harshly. The biggest religions are the most authoritarian.

When we first become aware of their subversiveness, we hate and we punish with the most extreme violence the mystic, the anarchist, the conscientious objector, and the heretic, who all in one way or another question our ancient systems of domination. The mystic eroticizes, deconstructs, or demythologizes the language of domination, in order – perhaps by *disarming* God, as the harlot disarmed Enkidu[4] – to make God lovable. The apostate tries to escape domination. The anarchist, the draft-dodger and the anti-war protester question whether it is right that in a popular democracy the State should still claim the power and authority of an absolute monarch over young people of military age. In the period of the Vietnam war draft, young Americans who had been brought up to believe themselves citizens found that they were not citizens at all, but subjects pressed into the service of an all-powerful sovereign. They were shocked at being forced to recognize that even in America humanity's ancient nightmare has not yet been exorcized.

It is sometimes said that the First World War sealed the Death of God in Europe, and people suggest that the reason for this was that the evils and suffering of the period were so great that in the face of them people could no longer believe in a loving God. This is a mistaken analysis: terrible hardship and suffering have always been most people's experience. Rather, we should think of the armies of young men going towards their deaths and asking themselves "Exactly *why* does all of human life have to be lived in subjection to a sovereign power that may at any time and for its own inscrutable purposes order *this* to happen?" The question is not one about the love of God, but about the sovereign authority of God and the State: shall we *always* have to live as people who are at the disposal of an unconditionally sovereign absolute Power? Will we *never* be entirely free? Are human beings not capable of freedom?

Against this background, and in the context of a vast change in consciousness now taking place, the mysticism of secondariness is a form of religious consciousness that is happy, and even cosmically *grateful*, to discover that one really can live without absolutes of any kind, in Heaven or on Earth. Traditionally-minded people think a fully horizontalized, democratic, and casually negotiated world will be unpleasantly lightweight. But I truly feel *religiously* happy about it, cosmically happy, happy even in suffering, happy to die. We don't actually *need* any kind of monarchy. It is enough for everything to be secondary, for everything to be relative, for everything to be sustained by no more than what Hume calls "custom" – mere informally negotiated habitual patterns of interaction and exchange. I am grateful for the sheer gratuitousness of everything. I feel spiritually liberated, cleansed, unaccountable, carefree, floating. That existence is purposeless is to me religiously wonderful. And because I know that life after death was not designed to be good news, but as a terrorist threat, I am very happy to be heading before very long into the bliss of extinction.

The Everlasting

The second leading attribute of God is his being everlasting. In the pre-Enlightenment vision of the world, time was seen almost solely as a destroyer and hardly ever as a creator. Time slipped away, time carried off: time was associated with change, disintegration, decline, loss, forgetfulness, deterioration, parting, and death. Happiness was sought by looking beyond things temporal to an unchanging eternal realm. One might look back to an Age of Gold in the time before time at the beginning of the world, or forward to an Age of Gold in the time after time at the end of the world. But as for the present, it was almost always seen as a period of decline. The empirical world was so unstable that there could be no sure knowledge of it, and no enduring values or standards could be grounded in it.

As a result, a certain alienation from the here and now was customary and even obligatory. Even today a person who lives wholly in the present – a person who goes with the flow and is fully committed to life – is spoken of disapprovingly as "materialistic." A bizarre word: perhaps its ultimate source is the saying in the Sermon of the Mount about laying up treasure for oneself in Heaven and not on Earth. Earthly, material goods are an unsound and risky investment. They decay and get stolen, whereas heavenly investment in non-material or spiritual goods is a completely secure investment. A materialist then is a foolish investor, a person who unwisely invests too heavily in the things of this world and the here and now, whereas a wise investor will think long-term and invest in the things of the spirit.

A series of contrasts have become built-in, and they overlap strikingly. The things of the flesh, material things, and the things of the spirit: the temporal and the spiritual, the proximate and the ultimate, the shallow and the deep, the outer and the inner. And all these contrasts converged upon the one great contrast between the eternal, Everlasting God and the time-bound, perishing human self.

It may be claimed that all these (broadly) Platonic oppositions are dead now; but they are not, for the contrast between "materialism" and "spirituality" is still being made, and is still entering the language of the newest of New Age movements. And we need to be rid of it: for so long as we make the distinction between the changing and the unchanging, things temporal and things spiritual, we will continue to be ill-at-ease in time and to fear death. The more completely we come to see ourselves, our thinking, and our world as embedded in time, and as simply coinciding with our own flowing temporality, the less we will wish to clutch at supposedly non-temporal fixed points outside life. There are none. *Panta rei*, everything flows.

Everything is contingent, everything is temporal, everything is part of the flux of becoming, everything pours out and passes away, including not only us and our world, but also our language, our knowledge, our values, our standards, and our gods. Holding on is an illusion: there is nothing to hold on to.[5] All our loves are slipping away at just the same speed as we are, and we should be happy to go along with them. I become completely happy about my own temporality when I understand that temporality is radically outsideless. Linguistic meaning, expressed truth, thought – all depend upon temporal succession, and therefore everything does. Time conditions everything: like a river our life runs down, and out into the sea.

Consider, for example, how the meaning of a spoken word hasn't fully arrived until the speech-act to which it contributes is complete – by which time the word itself has gone. That's secondariness: all meaning arrives a little belatedly. We have to slip away all the time in order fully to come. All life's like that, and so is consciousness, and so is art. Everything comes fully to itself only in retrospect. There's a profound interweaving of going and coming, dying and living, loss and gain, so that when I have fully accepted and affirmed my own temporality, I have said Yes to death and am happy. To have said Yes to life is also to have said Yes to death.

And God? Giving up the realistic metaphysical idea of God as an all-powerful timeless superperson, I come instead to see God as being more like a dead person, someone who has become complete and fully himself in death, someone who, like my other dead mentors and constant companions, is with me always in virtue of his absence in death. In death, united with God, we shall have become finally and unchangeably ourselves.

*   *   *   *

I have been using the phrase "religious happiness" as an alternative to the older term "salvation," and have been describing the mysticism of secondariness as a path to religious happiness. On the negative side, this happiness arises as we find ourselves at last liberated from two of humankind's worst and most ancient terrors. The first of these, as we have seen, is the fear that human nature is so wayward and wicked that human beings will always need to be terrified into subdued behaviour by a system of unlimited spiritual domination. Bizarre, that for millennia it was considered that the only way life could be made worth living was by terrifying people so much that their life *wasn't* worth living. The second terror is the ancient mistrust and fear of our own temporality, which has had the effect of alienating us from our own lives, and has led us to waste our energies in pursuing illusions of timelessness, and in fighting the passing of the years.

There is great happiness in being liberated from these two terrors. Everything is temporally conditioned, everything is secondary, everything is invented, everything comes and goes, everything comes fully to itself only belatedly or in retrospect, and there's nothing to complain about, and nobody to complain to. True, the world is much lighter than we thought, but that is a blessed relief. We don't in fact need to live under domination, and temporality has no outside. Since all meaning and truth, language and thought are temporally conditioned, the whole idea of jumping clear of time is empty. Besides, what is *wrong* with time, anyway? Time always and everywhere brings gain as well as loss, creation as well as destruction, and life as well as death. In secondariness, the opposites are always interwoven. Surprisingly, one finds oneself very happy to buy the package.

Cassandras all around us, some of them academic conservatives and rationalists, and some of them religious and political conservatives, have made "relativism" and "nihilism" into boowords. But let us not get involved with trying to rehabilitate words that have been sullied. Let us instead press on to describe how the mysticism of secondariness is a vision of the world that also generates a positive happiness of its own.

The Fountain

I have been describing mystical writing as a deconstructive kind of writing that works to break down the structures of religious alienation that the various "orthodoxies" have entrenched in our language. Orthodox theism in particular sets up the religious object as God, infinite, transcendent, objective, very close to us, but incomprehensible by us and quite inaccessible except via a certain very complex apparatus of mediation . . . and so on. In short, systems of metaphysical and religious belief always put the Object that our heart desires at some distance from us – perhaps in a better world – and so serve the interests of the expert guides or mediators who can help us to get to that better place. But the mystical writer wants to encourage us to believe instead that "God can be known immediately." This is achieved in writing by describing the religious life, and especially the practice of meditation and contemplative prayer. In prolonged meditation we learn to relax the linguistic special training and the effort of will by which in ordinary speech substances are composed, hierarchies of power confirmed, and value-scales established. The metaphysical structures crumple and collapse downwards. Everything slowly subsides and flattens out into a depthless continuum of flowing meanings. The "I" melts down into the continuum, and so too does God. So God and the self are united at last, in their mutual dissolution. This is the meaning of the old devotional phrase, "we in him and he in us." The "I" becomes, as the beautiful phrase has it, "lost in thought," entranced, absorbed. One begins to feel happier and happier as one dissolves. That's meditation: the flattening out and the dissemination *heal* the mind. *Try* it!

Here is a parallel example. Orthodox science works with a particular kind of realist epistemology classically established by René Descartes. The scientist is strictly trained to view him or herself as, and to write in the person of, a disembodied and rather abstract ideal observer who (oddly) still has sense organs to observe with even though disembodied. The whole world of subjectivity becomes a curiously empty inner space within which a diagrammatic representation of external, physical reality is constructed.

Just in order to work, then, the scientist is required to be inwardly somewhat distanced from his or her own feeling-life, and to regard the mental world within which scientific knowledge is constructed and held as being a distinct world, quite different in kind from the world of physical Nature. But yet at the same time the scientist's own theory tells her that she has herself emerged from and remains integrally a part of the very world that she's copying in knowledge. Training and practice, in the life sciences especially, may thus have the double effect of both creating and also calling into question an uncomfortable feeling of alienation from the natural world, and one can well see why many scientists seek relief in various kinds of nature-mysticism and Green activism. It is very agreeable to dissolve yourself back into the realm from which your professional discipline has distanced you out.

Mystical writing of any kind, then, is therapeutic. It seeks to cure the deep feeling of alienation that is produced by perhaps every professional discipline, and by institutionalization. Mystical writing, like the deconstruction of which it is the forerunner, has the effect of dismantling all substances, hierarchies, scales, and foundations, and so melting everything down into immanence – a one-level floating continuum. Everything, including the self, disappears into shimmering oceanic bliss, beginningless, endless, foundationless, secondariness. This is the Unitive State, the Spiritual Marriage, "the Real."

From this perspective, what is the religious object now seen to be? It is something that Heidegger calls Be-ing or E-vent, which is (roughly) all existence seen as continuous temporal process, as Becoming, or Forthcoming. Since the only Be-ing of which we are directly aware is our own human process of Be-ing, *Dasein*, what we call Be-ing is very close to what we call "Life." To make it religiously accessible, I propose that we picture it as the Fountain. Seen from a distance, a waterfall or a fountain may appear still and peaceful; but as we draw very close to them it becomes more and more apparent that what appeared stationary is in fact nothing but an outrush of pure formless contingency that is continuously renewed. Now draw back again and watch. Meditate. The fountain or the falls become again a traditional symbol of life's, or time's, perpetual self-renewal, a symbol of healing, refreshment, and repose.

There are objects that flit away extremely fast, as fast as light, as fast as time, so fast that they continuously and evenly replace themselves and appear to be very calm and still. Because they seem so still, many philosophers have sought to explain the persisting identity of objects through time in causal terms. Its state at t_0 causes its state at t_1, and so on: it is as if the object, in flitting away all the time, also continuously replaces itself. But this continuing extremely rapid self-replacement betrays itself by a certain faint shimmering, iridescence, trembling. And of that the Fountain is an image.[6] To me at least, that shimmering is the Sacred.

From this perspective, how are we now to explain religious happiness? According to Plato and the rationalist tradition, because we are ourselves rational beings, our highest happiness is to be found in the timeless contemplation of eternal necessity of being. According to Aristotle and the more mundane and "social" tradition, because we are ourselves complex, social beings with a whole range of capacities, our highest happiness is to be found in virtuous activity. (Aristotle continues also to pay lip-service to the contemplative ideal, but it is only lip-service.)

Here a different view is being put forward. All existence is seen as a self-renewing, endlessly outpouring continuous stream of minute scattering energies-read-as-signs. Everything is contingent, and it-all – "the Whole" is rather too reifying an expression – it-all is outsideless.

We can arrive at this vision of the world just through *religious meditation*, whether by loving God or by *zazen*. We can arrive at this vision of the world by *philosophical analysis*. We can arrive at this vision of the world by the practice of *deconstruction*, which eventually reduces everything to an endless streaming play of signs. We can arrive at a version of this vision of the world by the study of the *physical sciences*, which may be seen as reducing all of Nature to a dance of minute mathematical patterns. We may arrive at a version of this vision of the world by the study of the *biological sciences*, and in particular by becoming enraptured at life's ability endlessly both to replicate itself and to vary itself, and by life's combination of utter fragility with unstoppable tenacity. We may arrive at this vision of the world just by way of becoming absorbed in *music*, in *painting* or in the superabundant communicative life of humankind in the *media* age.

Moralists and rationalists are wont to denounce relativism, the endlessness of secondariness. But it can enrapture critics, designers, and specialist collectors – just as a single text, for example, seems to contain endless possibilities of interpretation; and I knew a man (a well-known figure; did you know him?) with a truly wonderful collection of *moustache-cups*.

At any rate, when meditation or critical thinking or both have brought everything down into secondariness, and when we have become fully aware both of language and of temporality, our vision of the world enfolds within itself this text as it is being written, together with the author as he writes it and you as you read it. And the religious object is now seen to be the disappearance of us all and of everything into shimmering oceanic bliss; beginningless, endless, foundationless, outsidelessness, and eternally transient secondariness: the Fountain, the new god, the true god, our happiness.

A Parthian shot. Classical mysticism felt the need to deconstruct classical ontotheology because it was so oppressively *heavy*. The mysticism of secondariness rather similarly reacts against today's talk about how much we need "meaning" and "purpose," as if what we really want is to spend all eternity working nonstop for the biggest Boss of all. No: taking a hint from Eckhart, I'll fasten on that impeccably orthodox word "Grace," and I'll teach that the highest religious happiness lies in the Graciousness of sheer gratuitousness.

The Saving Word

In Modern thinking, especially between the seventeenth and the early twentieth centuries, factually true sentences were widely thought of as matching or corresponding to objective facts. That is to say that when we tell the truth about some matter of fact, the sentences we produce somehow manage to copy, track, or mirror the shapes of the states of things that we are describing.

Even today, many idioms in common use still imply that when a person tells the truth, there is a point-by-point correspondence or isomorphism between what is said and what is the case. Yet those few philosophers who have tried to make this notion precise have come up against extraordinary difficulties. Exactly *how* does a string of noises or marks manage to be a realistic portrait of a state of affairs? Or conversely, what is it about the structure of the world around us that *makes* it copyable in human language? What *are* these two shapes, the shape of a state of affairs and the shape of a true sentence, that one of them can resemble or be a copy of the other?

The last and boldest attempt, by people of the very highest ability, to answer these questions was made by Russell and the young Wittgenstein in the first quarter of the twentieth century.[7] As is well known, Wittgenstein's solution in the *Tractatus* required him to work with very austere and stripped-down conceptions both of the world and of the scope of philosophy. In effect, the price to be paid for learning how it is possible to state a fact was the realization that nothing else can be said. The self, theology, ethics, and art all drop out of language. They all become "mystical." Following Schopenhauer, Wittgenstein at this early stage in his career used the term "the mystical" to refer to matters which are of great importance but which cannot be put into words.

In the following years it became clear that, even within the extremely restricted area left to him, Wittgenstein still had not by any means achieved a fully satisfactory solution to his problems. So, after Wittgenstein, philosophy began finally to give up realism. At the very least, it is obvious that language is used for many other purposes than fact-stating: it is used, for example, to greet people, to establish accord with them, and to secure cooperation with them. It is used in all sorts of ways to express, declare, or advertise our own needs, feelings, and intentions; it is used to warn, to command, to request, and to woo. In short, we use language in a great variety of conventional ways to negotiate our relationships with each other and to express ourselves. And by thus directing attention to the practical and expressive uses of language, we connect it better with the rich and varied animal communication-systems out of which it has presumably evolved. And indeed the animal examples suggest that there could be, and perhaps have been, complete functioning and biologically adequate languages in which the purely descriptive use of language hardly figured at all.

So far, so good: but it is still necessary to explain how descriptive language is possible and how it works. If we refer back now to an earlier stage in this present argument, we can pick out a vital clue. I asked: "What is it about the structure of the world that makes it copyable in human language?" At least in the English puritan and liberalist tradition, the answer is clear: we were first created and given the power of speech by God, who himself used language when he formed the world. So God made the world language-shaped, and when we use descriptive language in a rigorously truthful way we are tracking God's work. Herein lies the connection between Calvinism, truthfulness, and the rise of empirical science. Here is an example of a Victorian puritan making the point:

> there is no training more necessary for children than that of teaching them not merely to speak the truth in the ordinary vulgar sense of the term, but to speak it in a much higher sense, by rigidly compelling, point by point, a correspondence of the words with the fact external or internal.[8]

A good Christian lives literally and punctiliously according to the text of scripture, and if life can thus be strictly conformed to text, so, in the opposite direction, language can equally strictly be made to conform to the facts.

In the seventeenth century these ideas were developed in the famous doctrine of the Two Books, Nature and Scripture. God has written the Book of Scripture in words, and we copy it out in our lives. God has written the Book of Nature in creatures and in numerical patterns, and we copy it out in our descriptions and mathematical equations that track his mind. Again we see how the rise of Modern science depended upon borrowing from the older world-view the belief that the world has been expressly made to be intelligible and describable by us, and in our language.[9]

In which case, we see how the doctrine that language doesn't just copy reality, but actually *determines* it, is very far from being merely a questionable innovation of recent years. On the contrary, it is a very old idea, found in creation-myths across both the Old and the New Worlds,[10] and perhaps essential to thought. If we give up the realist idea that a benevolent (and talkative) Creator has set up, once and for all, a pre-established harmony between language and reality, the only remaining possibility surely is that we ourselves must be constantly using and developing our language to differentiate the continuum of experience, to divide up the world, and to give the world its structure. We ourselves are continually building our own various human worlds – or, better: in our expressive use of language we get ourselves together, and in our descriptive use of language we are given our world.

To take these in turn, and very briefly: a human being is a microcosm, that is, a little fountain, a system of natural energies that are often somewhat at odds with each other, and are struggling to pour out into expression. Linguistic and other signs provide potential outlets, and have the power to allow several different forces to express themselves at once. Naturally, we are easiest with those forms of expression through which we can best get ourselves together and express ourselves most completely in the most unified manner. Thus, all human expressive activity has the character of art, and (as has been said earlier) we come to ourselves, and fully become ourselves, only a little belatedly, in expression and as we pass away. We are solar, burning away, racing towards our own fulfilment and most complete expression in death. The big O.

What I have called language, religion calls the Word. It is a saving, redeeming word insofar as it draws us out into reconciled, unified expression. The Word lures us out into a dying life through which we become ourselves *in passing*.

In the mysticism of secondariness language is spoken of as creative and redemptive in another sense. We must give up the idea that we are the masters of our own language. We don't create ourselves or build our world all by ourselves. Language tempts us out into expression, gives us ourselves, offers us more possible worlds than we will ever be able to count or to try out. We have to learn the trick of letting language speak, letting language do the talking, letting language create.[11] And to feel oneself thus upborne by language – that is mystical.

CHAPTER TEN

eternity

On August 2, 1844 the poet John Clare wrote "A Vision" in the General Lunatic Asylum at Northampton, England. He had already been three years certified insane, and in declining health for over twenty years. Yet poetical language surging through him could still rouse him to an exalted and joyous mood:

> I lost the love of heaven above,
> I spurned the lust of earth below,
> I felt the sweets of fancied love
> And hell itself my only foe.
>
> I lost earth's joys, but felt the glow
> Of heaven's flame abound in me,
> Till loveliness, and I, did grow
> The bard of immortality.
>
> I loved but woman fell away,
> I hid me from her faded fame,
> I snatch'd the sun's eternal ray
> And wrote till earth was but a name.
>
> In every language upon earth,
> On every shore, o'er every sea,
> I gave my name immortal birth
> And kept my spirit with the free.[1]

Clare was not an educated man, and is not usually seen as being a religious poet at all; but these few verses contain a great deal of traditional religious vocabulary. He sings of Heaven and Hell, love and lust, the immortal and the eternal, and spirit; and he is using this vocabulary in what was then a rather novel expressive and emotive way.

Take, for example, the notion of eternity. In those canonical poets who make the most use of the word – one thinks mainly of *Hamlet*, of Marvel and Vaughan, and even of Shelley – the word "eternity" still carries its old associations with Plato's world of timeless Forms, and in religion with God's timeless Being, with life after death and the heavenly world. But in Clare's very post-Platonic and Romantic use of the word, eternity has come to be associated much more with this world and with the forces of nature. It is associated with a soaring, cosmic religious feeling that is no longer tied to any particular philosophical doctrine or system of religious belief. It has become expressive rather than descriptive.

To say this seems to put Clare in a tradition that runs from Wordsworth and Turner through to the 1880s and Nietzsche, in whom the new sense of eternity becomes most fully developed. The eternal is linked with the Sun, and with the "dynamical sublime" in Nature. The old theological topic of the soul's relation to God has been transposed into a new key, involving a much more bodily and more emotional response to Nature and to natural forces.

But there is more to be said than that, for what is most striking in Clare's poem is that he has "snatch'd the sun's eternal ray" in order to *write* with it. He experiences his own poetic gift as being itself a force of Nature, a burning solar fire within himself that flares up and demands expression in poetical writing. In Clare's poetry, language and Nature are deeply interwoven: all Nature whispers to him, he writes all Nature.[2]

It is a commonplace that in the great writers and artists of the nineteenth century we witness migrations of the sacred, from religion into Nature, and from religion into art. But Clare gives us a little more than that. His answer to the popular late-Modern question, "What is the mystical? Where can we now locate it?" is that the mystical is the way poetic language streams over, forms, and enfolds the entire empirical world. And that is something that any of us may *feel*, in our own perception and our own speech and writing.

The old eternal world, whether the philosophers' world of Forms and eternal truths or the heavenly world of religion, had always been regarded as an *unchanging* world. It was omnipresent. It enfolded the empirical world and made everything intelligible. But in traditional society it was always seen as being changeless; whereas the new supernatural world is the world of language, a highly energetic world of dancing signs. It is the true successor of the old world of forms. It does the same job and occupies the same place. But it is notably different. Its constituents are not abstract notions, clear-cut and transparent to reason, but words and other signs – shimmering, ambiguous, mutable, and subject to all sorts of delays, reversals, and transformations. Words? Their name is Legion, says the unfortunate demoniac in the Gospel, who evidently knew what it's like to be a writer.

Religion has changed accordingly. In the old supernatural world, the most appropriate religious activity was the calm rational contemplation of timeless verities. In the new supernatural world perhaps the very highest religious happiness is to *surf* language. John Clare's new and post-metaphysical use of "eternity" expresses his solar joy in surfing poetic language as he writes. In him one sees religion becoming less of a distinct sacred sphere of life, and instead something that is more general, cosmic, and expressive. Religious thanksgiving, for example, becomes a new "open" or non-objective feeling of cosmic gratitude. One feels generally grateful to everything for everything. Religious joy is now that exultant joy in surfing language. Religious worship has become a feeling of awe, sometimes tinged with a sense of unworthiness, that one may experience before sublimity or grandeur in Nature or art. There are some high viewpoints at which one may suddenly desire to plunge forwards and down, and die into what is before one's eyes; and the feeling is subjectively indistinguishable from the old intense desire – do you remember it? – to drown in God. But what is its object? It is object*less* – just as religious love is now a non-objective universal loving attitude. To "love God" is just to love non-objectively. Clare does, of course, have particular love-objects, and notably his Mary. But his love for Mary is not fixated, idolatrous, or exclusive: it broadens out, to become also a universal objectless world-love.

Religious feeling, I am suggesting, has become democratized, spread around. It is e-motion, a movement outwards, and indeed the word "emotion" could at one time be used to mean migration. Religious e-motion is outpouring feeling.[3] It is self-abandonment, cosmic, solar, and non-objective – which means not focusing and fastening upon any particular object. Formed by language, this feeling may speak words of gratitude, love, joy, and adoration. It may use a good deal of the old religious vocabulary. It may even speak of God; but not because God is a being. God too is cosmic and non-objective: that is, the word "God" is poetical, signifying the non-objective object of religious feeling, that to which one's heart goes out. Notice that when an ordinary person, perhaps in shock or in admiration, says *sotto voce* "Oh God!" the word "God" functions simply and only as an exclamation. It is a catalyst for the expression of religious feeling or perhaps the vehicle that carries an expressed feeling, but it is no more than that.

Such an exclamatory use of the word "God" is at least reasonably clean and honest. It makes sense. God is Everything, Nothing, It-all, and even, as we say, "Nothing in particular."

That the words "God," "All," and "Nothing" are more or less interchangeable has often been noticed by religious writers.[4] An excellent example of a thoroughly "non-cognitive" or "non-realist" mystical writer is the author of *The Cloud of Unknowing*, a small English treatise of the fourteenth century. He is entirely serious about his title. He really means his Negative Theology. God is loved, not known. "The highest and next way to heaven is run by desires and not by paces of feet" (chapter 60).[5] As for the object of religious aspiration, it is nowhere and nought (68). It makes us nowhere and nought, too, indeed: our wits cannot reason about it – but that only makes us love it all the more. God's emptiness has the effect of purifying and intensifying religious feeling to the highest degree. That is to say, for the author of the *Cloud*, the very fact that God isn't out-there and doesn't literally exist is necessary if we are to learn a truly religious, non-objective, solar, disinterested, and divine sort of love.

But if a God who isn't really there has taught that kind of love for the first time, it is as if our soul has been blinded by the intensity of our feeling, blinded "for abundance of ghostly light," and we may then call the religious object All.

Thus the words "God," "Nothing," and "All" are equivalent, and the *Cloud* author does indeed present a non-cognitive and purely e-motive view of religion. Or at least, the author has left us a text that is wide open to such a reading. It is obvious – so obvious that apparently nobody can see it. Partly the problem has been that the past two millennia and more of metaphysics have not yet been shaken off. They still have us badly misreading mystical texts. So much is this the case that – as we saw when discussing Eckhart – even Derrida, who is normally pretty acute, thinks that the Negative Theology still remains within metaphysics. Not in the *Cloud*, it doesn't. The Negative Theology, deriving from Plotinus and the pseudo-Dionysius, really is wanting to cure us of the bad old intellectualist habit of always putting the question of speculative truth first, always wanting to get back in the end to some form of theological realism. The *Cloud* author seeks to cure us for ever. Why can't we see it? No doubt we are again misled here by the late-Modern relaunch of the mystics as orthodox apologists. People simply cannot credit that the *Cloud* author actually held (or, at any rate, has not precluded) the sort of non-realist views for which certain contemporary theologians have become notorious.

Nevertheless, for the negative theologian, realism must involve a form of "idolatry" – idolatry meaning the *fixation* of religious feeling upon an object, this and not-that. Genuine faith is not fixated at all; it is "open," solar, cosmic, non-objective, and universal feeling pouring out into expression. "God" is just a non-objective symbol that evokes religious feeling, or a vehicle that carries it; and as such the word "God" is interchangeable with a number of other words that do the same job in other traditions.

This religious equivalence of a variety of different terms which may seem to be opposites is delightfully exemplified in Japanese Buddhism, where people like to play upon the similarity of the words *u*, *mu*, and *ku*. You may use in meditation one of these words, dashingly penned by a Zen monk who is a calligrapher. *U* is Being, *mu* is Nothingness, and *ku* is Emptiness. In Mahayana Buddhism, Emptiness is *sunyata*, the insubstantiality of everything, and it is said to be "skylike," the sky being non-objective in such a way that one might perhaps see it either as a plenum or as absolutely void.

A similar coincidence of opposites in the religious object is more common in the Bible than many people have noticed. God, for example, dwells *both* in unapproachably dazzling light, *and* in deep darkness. Henry Vaughan combines the two arrestingly in the phrase "dazzling darkness."[6]

This deliberate use of paradox is intended to teach non-realism. We are being warned not to try to theorize such language or to understand it in metaphysical or "realist" terms. Such ways of thinking are useless and even harmful.

A clear parallel case is that of UFOs. UFOs are not things-out-there. UFOs are merely a class of reported events not yet filed in any particular category. So UFO is a negative term. One shouldn't objectify UFOs – but of course people want to objectify, and others perceive a chance to profit by their credulity. Maybe it doesn't very much matter that some people do objectify UFOs, and that ufology is a profitable business. But it does matter that people objectify God and that huge and highly exploitative religious systems profit by their credulity. And once such a system is established, it has a vested interest in keeping people credulous.

Here, we do not objectify. We stay with the mystics Eastern and Western, and notice the striking way that certain ambivalent and very general religious signs attract the outpouring of religious feeling, *and work all the better just because of their very ambivalence.*

There is here a close parallel with art. The best art often attracts stronger feeling precisely because it is compressed, ambivalent, and open to a range of different interpretations. Like a joke, it is spoiled if it is over-explained. It needs to be both deep and light.

An example: the British land artist Andy Goldsworthy (b. 1956) creates works of art out of natural materials only. He usually works in the open air, picking up the leaves, stones, branches, and so forth that come to hand. Sometimes he builds installations in galleries, and in 1992–3 did so in city museums first in California and then later in Japan.[7] These works consisted of very light and fragile screens or curtains, crossing a whole room in the gallery. Each was a delicate lattice of individual stems of grass or rush, pinned together with thorns. At one point the stems were so arranged as to form tangents around an empty circular hole or void in the screen.

So what do these beautiful works "mean"? What is the hole; why is it there? Goldsworthy is usually assumed to be exploring Nature, natural forces and energies. An environmentalist might think of the hole as the Sun, which sustains the delicate veil of plant life wrapped around the globe. An American Christian might think of the hole as signifying an unrepresentable transcendent Creator of all life. You cannot make a picture of him out of twigs and stalks, but you can arrange twigs and stalks in such a way as to hint at the shape of his absence. A Japanese viewer, on the other hand, is sure to see the work as most beautifully teaching the principles of Buddhism. The delicate gauzy curtain of plant materials speaks of the insubstantiality of the entire world of being-born and dying, and the hole speaks of *mu*, the blissful Void, absolute Nothingness. The Japanese viewer will also note the fact that Goldsworthy's artworks are themselves very impermanent, universal Impermanence being a major theme of Buddhism. More insistently than Christianity, Buddhism says, "You can't take it with you. Let go. Let it go."

One could continue: our present point is simply that Goldsworthy's work is religious – that is, it is religiously moving, it attracts religious feeling, all the more strongly because of its extreme lightness and impermanence, its multiple meanings, and its capacity to say different things to different people.

Goldsworthy's work is not historical; but in our post-historical time I like that, and am conscious of differing from the very able Australian-American art critic Robert Hughes. Hughes is evidently a humanist, and very historically minded. He likes solid datable human warmth and complexity in his art, and is surely the sort of person for whom the best religious art is like that of medieval Christianity or Hinduism, in being packed with iconography highly specific to one particular tradition as it was at a certain place and time. For him, I think, religion needs to be solid and specific, and he has recently made some very disparaging remarks about the religious pretensions of the New York abstract expressionists in general, and Barnett Newman in particular.[8]

We come here to a parting of the ways. In the globalized post-history that we are now coming to inhabit, the old regional cultural and religious traditions have all stopped developing. In dying, they have become "heritage," "roots," "ethnicity," our national and religious "identity," an idealized past into which we continually return in order to restore our sense of self. Our own contemporary world is increasingly post-humanist, and to become the sort of selves we still want to be, we must keep returning into a mythical past (in Britain usually a mixture of the worlds of Jane Austen and the Ealing Studios).

Such is our popular right postmodernism, our local-tradition-fundamentalism. As a way of coping in the short term with the violent cultural change now sweeping the world, it is entirely understandable. But it cannot last. Soon the old local and pre-technological cultures will be lost to living memory. Already the world of the early nineteenth century is as remote as the Middle Ages, so far as most people are concerned.

What about the other way, that of left postmodernism? Increasingly we live in an ultralight and radically relativistic world in which there are no certainties, no fixed points, no absolutes. Everything is in ceaseless flux. Nothing is primary, everything is secondary: that is, everything is a transient construct. "Identity" is dead. The self cannot be more than a transient effect, real only *in passing*.

I have argued that the mysticism of secondariness actually *likes* this condition. The lighter and the more ambiguous our religious symbolism, the purer and the more ardent the expression of religious feeling becomes. In 1966, in the closing lines of his book *Les Mots et les choses*, Michel Foucault ominously threatened "the death of man."[9] Now that it has happened, I put on record the view that it can be experienced as an emotional and a religious liberation. The world passes away, the death of God is followed by the death of Man, the new right gets ever more irascible – and some of us find, perversely, that our hearts become warmer and our faith stronger.

notes

Introduction

1   See Mark C. Taylor, *Erring: a postmodern a/theology* (Chicago: Chicago University Press, 1984).

2   Thus Mary Warnock, although in many ways sympathetic to Don Cupitt's "consistently mythological" interpretation of religious belief, reacts sharply against his more postmodernist ideas, especially as they are put forward in *What is a Story?* (London: SCM Press, 1991). "What lies behind this," she says, "is plainly a galloping and, I believe, in the long run destructive relativism" (*Imagination and Time*, Oxford: Blackwell, 1984, p. 94). But I am here retorting that relativism is (sort of) true, and I *like* it. What relativism destroys, *needs* to be destroyed.

3   Thus William James: "mystical states seem to those who experience them to be also states of knowledge" (*The Varieties of Religious Experience*, 1902, Lect. XVI and XVII: "Mysticism," p. 380). Unlike later critics, James does not attack the contradiction in describing a state as being *both* "ineffable" *and* "noetic." On this latter point see, for example, Richard M. Gale, "Mysticism and philosophy," *Journal of Philosophy*, 57 (1960); reprinted in Steven M. Cahn and David Shatz (eds), *Contemporary Philosophy of Religion* (New York: Oxford University Press, 1982), pp. 113–22.

4   *Tractatus*, 6:44.

Chapter 1: The Modern Construction of Mysticism and Religious Experience

1   See, for example, Robert C. Solomon, *Continental Philosophy since 1750: the rise and fall of the self*, OPUS: A History of Western Philosophy, Vol. 7 (Oxford: Oxford University Press, 1988).

2   See particularly Descartes, *Meditations*, 6; and Locke's *Essay Concerning Human Understanding*, Book IV, 21.

3   Edward Craig, *The Mind of God and the Works of Man* (Oxford: Oxford University Press, 1987), pp. 22ff.

4   For example, Timothy Beardsworth, *A Sense of Presence* (Oxford: RERU, 1977); Edward Robinson, *The Original Vision* (Oxford: RERU,

1977); David Hay, *Exploring Inner Space*, revised edn (Oxford: A.R. Mowbray, 1987).

5   *Institutes*, I, 1, i.

6   Evidence in Michael Argyle and Benjamin Beit-Hallahmi, *The Social Psychology of Religion* (London: Routledge, 1975), pp. 89ff.: "among scientists and academicians psychologists are the least religious of all groups."

7   For example, *The Cloud of Unknowing*, 1–8. (See chap. 10, n. 5.)

8   For Islam, a faith that gets a poor press nowadays, the mystical tradition was well opened up by R.A. Nicholson, *Studies in Islamic Mysticism* (Cambridge: Cambridge University Press, 1921); and Margaret Smith, *Studies in Early Mysticism in the Near and Middle East*, 1931, reprinted as *The Way of the Mystics* (London: Sheldon Press, 1976).

9   *The World as Will and as Representation*, Vol. II, chap. 18. "A way *from within* stands open to us to that real inner nature of things to which we cannot penetrate *from without*. It is, so to speak, a subterranean passage, a secret alliance, which, as if by treachery, places us all at once in the fortress that could not be taken by attack from without . . ." (New York: Dover Publications edn of 1966), p. 195.

10   Don Cupitt, *Solar Ethics* (London: SCM Press, 1995).

11   My mentor complains that this is too schematic, and of course he's right. We are not talking just about distinct historical periods, but about styles of thinking that have coexisted among (and even within) us since the later Middle Ages. Postmodern aestheticism, stressing the primacy of art and the sign, goes back at least to the Romantics and Schelling; and conversely, today's mathematical Platonists are traditional Objective Rationalists. I periodize and polarize simply for the sake of clarity.

Chapter 2: Theories of Mysticism in Modernity

1   John Cook Wilson, *Statement and Inference* (Oxford: Clarendon Press, 1926), Vol. 2, pp. 858–65.

2   Richard Swinburne, *The Existence of God* (Oxford: Clarendon Press, 1979), chap. 13: "The argument from religious experience," pp. 244–76.

3   John Hick, *An Interpretation of Religion: human responses to the transcendent* (London: Macmillan, 1989), p. 350.

4   Ibid.

5 Ibid., pp. 205–8. Hick's arguments for realism seem to be equally applicable to belief in astrology, life after death for pet animals, spiritualism, etc.

6 John Locke, *An Essay Concerning Human Understanding*, Book II, 23, 2.

7 All this is well described in Mark C. Taylor, *Disfiguring: art, architecture and religion* (Chicago: Chicago University Press, 1992), chap. 2, pp. 17–47.

8 *The Varieties of Religious Experience* (1902), Lect. 1: in the early editions, pp. 9–13.

9 J.H. Leuba, *The Psychology of Religious Mysticism* (New York: Harcourt, Brace, 1925).

10 See J.N.D. Kelly, *Jerome: his life, writings and controversies* (London: Duckworth, 1975), p. 102.

11 See Rowan Williams, *The Wound of Knowledge: Christian spirituality from the New Testament to St John of the Cross* (London: Darton, Longman and Todd, 1979), pp. 108–15.

12 Ibid., p. 133.

Chapter 3: Dogmatic Theology is an Ideology of Absolute Spiritual Power

1 *Rechtgläubigkeit und Ketzerei im ältesten Christentum* (Tübingen, J.C.B. Mohr, 1934); Eng. trans. by Robert Craft et al. (Philadelphia: Fortress, 1971).

2 J.K. Elliott, *The Apocryphal New Testament* (Oxford: Clarendon Press, 1993).

3 Bart D. Ehrman, *The Orthodox Corruption of Scripture: the effect of early Christological controversies on the text of the New Testament* (Oxford: Clarendon Press, 1993).

4 Notice here the popular use of "a proposition" to mean an offer to do business. The implication again is that "sense" is *commercial* sense.

5 Ehrman calls this the "separationist" Christology: his chap. 3, pp. 119–65.

6 Another instructive example of licit and illicit inference is this: If the Son of God can also be called "God the Son," why can't the Mother of God be called "God the Mother"?

7 I should explain that I use this term – the Law, religious law – here and on p. 1 above, in the Lacanian sense. I'm referring to a set of very deep and ancient prohibitions etc. that are still constitutive of our personalities and are presumably of religious origin.

Chapter 4: Mysticism is a Kind of Writing

1 Alexander Chancellor, *Guardian*, October 24, 1996.
2 W.T. Stace, *Mysticism and Philosophy* (Philadelphia: J.P. Lippincott, 1960; London: Macmillan, 1961).
3 Argyle and Beit-Hallahmi (cited above, chap. 1, n. 6), pp. 49f.; and Stace, pp. 110f.
4 Ibid., p. 50.
5 E.g., John Hick, *Faith and Knowledge*, 2nd edn (Ithaca: Cornell University Press, 1966), chap. 8.
6 Margaret Smith, *The Way of the Mystics: the early Christian mystics and the rise of the Sufis* (London: Sheldon Press, 1976), pp. 185–8, 218–25.
7 See A.K. Ramanujan, *Speaking of Siva* (Harmondsworth: Penguin, 1973), pp.19ff. The numbering is that of Basavanna's poems in the standard edition by S.S. Basavanal (Dharwar, 1962). Similarly, for Mahādēvi the numbering comes from L. Basavaraju (Mysore, 1966).
8 Alluding here to an astonishingly fine but sexually and politically dated lyric by Tennyson, "Summer Night," whose first line is "Now sleeps the crimson petal, now the white." The last eight lines run:

> Now lies the Earth all Danaë to the stars,
> And all thy heart lies open unto me.
> Now slides the silent meteor on, and leaves
> A shining furrow, as thy thoughts in me.
> Now folds the lily all her sweetness up,
> And slips into the bosom of the lake:
> So fold thyself, my dearest, thou, and slip
> Into my bosom and be lost in me.

Beautiful though they are, these lines are written from precisely the sexual-political standpoint that Mahādēvi, and mystical writing generally, are careful to shun. Tennyson identifies with a patriarchal male observer of Woman, who sees her as his private property, his fertile acres, his landscape. He is so self-assured that he can without any touch of irony address her as his cherished child, his devotee, and enjoin her to lose herself in him.

But notice that from the non-realist and postmodern standpoint we are all of us, men and women alike, always in language, always in secondariness, cosmically always in the female persona. We lose ourselves into universal and outsideless *différance* and secondariness. We are not in a position to know of any founding or cosmic monarchical maleness that transcends the entire field of *différance,* and into which we can lose ourselves. The very nature of language keeps any such figure permanently out of reach.

The mysticism of secondariness recognizes that, for all of us alike, Woman is symbolically the language, the *différance* and the secondariness from which we all arise and into which we all sink back and drown.

Chapter 5: How Mystical Writing Produces Religious Happiness

1   Cited from H.P. Cooke and Hugh Tredinnick, Aristotle: *The Organon I: The Categories, On Interpretation, The Prior Analytics* (London and Cambridge, MA: Loeb, 1938), p. 115.
2   Ibid.
3   *Paradiso,* XX, 79–81.
4   John Locke, *An Essay Concerning Human Understanding* (1690) Book III, 1, 2; 2, 2, etc.
5   Augustine, *Confessions,* Book Nine, X, 24: Library of Christian Classics edn, tr. A.C. Outler, 1955, p. 193.
6   Ibid., Book Seven, XVII, 23, with Outler's footnote discussion, pp. 151f.
7   J.M. Cohen (ed.), *The Penguin Book of Spanish Verse* (London: Penguin, 1956), pp. 179–81. I have taken out the capitalization of the first letters of "He" and "Him" in stanzas 6 and 7 of the translation.
8   A.A. Parker, *The Philosophy of Love in Spanish Literature* (Edinburgh: Edinburgh University Press, 1985), p. 88.
9   Ibid., pp. 77ff.
10   Ibid., pp. 94f.
11   Ibid., pp. 228f.
12   Ibid., p. 99, and n. 30 on p. 229.

Chapter 6: The Politics of Mysticism

1   See Emilie Zum Brunn, "Self, not-self and the ultimate in Marguerite Porete's 'Mirror of Annihilated Souls'"; in Robert E. Carter (ed.), *God, the Self and Nothingness: reflections Eastern and Western* (New York: Paragon House, 1990), pp. 81–7.
2   K.E. Kirk, *The Vision of God: the Christian doctrine of the summum bonum* (London: Longmans, Green, 1931), pp. 431–8.

3   Ibid., p. 437.

4   Ibid., p. 438, n. 1.

5   On this see the classic works by Mary Douglas: *Purity and Danger* (1966: latest reprints, London and New York: Routledge ARK edition, 1984, etc.); and *Natural Symbols* (1970: repr. Harmondsworth: Penguin, 1973, etc.).

6   Daphne Hampson, *Theology and Feminism* (Oxford: Blackwell, 1990); *After Christianity* (London: SCM Press, 1996). In the latter, see, e.g., p. 170.

7   For Thérèse, see (for example) *The Collected Letters of St Thérèse of Lisieux*, tr. F.J. Sheed (London: Sheed and Ward, 1949; reprinted in paper covers, 1977, 1979). The more recent names most often quoted are St Charles de Foucault and Thomas Merton, but the decline of the Church's coercive power has now largely – or, at least, partly – removed mystical writing's *raison d'être*.

8   *Judges* 17:6, 18:1, 19:1, 21:25.

9   See Richard Dawkins, *The Blind Watchmaker* (New York: W.W. Norton, 1986); *The Selfish Gene*, new edn (New York: Oxford University Press, 1989); *River out of Eden* (London: Weidenfeld and Nicolson; New York: Basic Books, 1995); and *Climbing Mount Improbable* (London: Viking Penguin, 1996).

Chapter 7: Mystical Writing was the Forerunner of Deconstruction and Radical Theology

1   In what follows I cite an old but much-liked edition of (most of) Eckhart's sadly small surviving corpus: Raymond B. Blakney, *Meister Eckhart: a modern translation* (New York: Harper Torchbooks, 1957).

2   John D. Caputo, "Mysticism and transgression: Derrida and Meister Eckhart," in Hugh J. Silverman (ed.), *Continental Philosophy III: Derrida and deconstruction* (New York and London: Routledge, 1989), pp. 24–39.

3   Blakney, p. 222.

4   Ibid.

5   Jacques Derrida, *Writing and Difference*, tr. Alan Bass (London: Routledge, 1978), p. 146.

6   Blakney, p. 229.

7   Ibid., p. 204.

8   For Derrida on Negative Theology and Eckhart see (in addition to the passage cited above) another passage in *Writing and Difference*, p. 337, n. 37; and the first essay in *Margins of Philosophy*, tr. Alan

Bass (Chicago: Chicago University Press, 1982); and "How to Avoid Speaking: Denials," in S. Budick and W. Iser (eds), *Languages of the Unsayable* (New York: Columbia University Press, 1989), pp. 3–70.

9   Blakney, p. 241 (Fr. 23); cf. p. 242 (Fr. 24).

10 Ibid., p. 248.

11 Ibid., p. 219.

12 Ibid., p. 180.

13 On all this, see Kevin Hart, *The Trespass of the Sign: deconstruction, theology and philosophy* (Cambridge: Cambridge University Press, 1989), especially pp. 255–7.

14 Heidegger gave a course of lectures on Eckhart at Freiburg in 1919.

15 Caputo (cited above, n. 2), p. 35.

16 Boethius, *The Consolation of Philosophy*, Pt V, 6.

17 *Confessions*, Book Eleven, XIII, 16; quoted from the Outler translation cited above, chap. 5, n. 5.

18 Blakney, p. 182 (amended slightly).

19 Ibid., p. 209. See also p. 212.

20 Ibid., p. 207.

Chapter 8: Meltdown

1   Bernard McGinn, *The Presence of God: a history of Western Christian mysticism, Volume 1: The Foundations of Mysticism* (London: SCM Press, 1992); Michel de Certeau, *The Mystic Fable, Volume 1: Sixteenth and Seventeenth Centuries*, published in French, Paris, 1982; trans. by Michael B. Smith (Chicago: Chicago University Press, 1992).

2   Ibid., pp. 108ff.

3   Elaine Pagels, *The Gnostic Gospels* (New York: Random House, 1979).

4   De Certeau, op. cit., pp. 1–3.

5   See above, p. 68.

6   Above, p. 65.

7   Cited from H. Bettenson (ed.), *Documents of the Christian Church* (Oxford: Oxford University Press, 1943), p. 71. Bettenson was my first theology teacher, and is here recalled with due *pietas*.

8   Ibid., p. 73.

9   Ibid., p. 65.

10 In the Middle Ages, theologians met the difficulty by arguing that souls in Heaven, like mystics on Earth in "infused contemplation," are in a state of rapture or ecstasy in which they are able like the angels to know "intelligible species" – in effect, the Platonic Forms – by direct intuition. Roughly, then, the answer is

that at least the angels know God, so if human souls in Heaven are supposed to be enjoying the Vision of God, it must be that they have been raised up to share in the angelic mode of cognition. On all this see, for example, K.E. Kirk, *The Vision of God* (cited, chap. 6, n. 2), note 5, pp. 548ff.

But this is not a satisfactory answer. Even if, for the sake of argument, we grant that there are angels, how can even they know a God who really is infinite and simple? It has always been recognized that an *infinite* God must transcend the categories of *any* finite understanding, angelic or not.

All Aquinas can really claim, on his own premises, is not that an actual infinite Being can *as such* be known by a finite mind, but rather and more modestly that angels and human souls in beatitude can understand everything "in God." A perspectiveless vision of reality can be enjoyed. One can know all the reasons why everything that is so, is so and cannot be otherwise, and in that God's-eye view of things we can be truly happy.

By implication, at least, Aquinas has to reduce "We can know and love God absolutely" to "We can know and love all things *in God*." This conclusion was finally drawn by Spinoza, whose philosophy is on the hinge between the old theological realist claim: "Our last end and supreme happiness is to know God and enjoy him forever," and the modern physical cosmologist's claim: "We'll be happy when we have a Grand Unified Theory of Everything, and so a complete fundamental science of nature."

11 I refer in particular to her poems.
12 R.A. Nicholson (cited above, chap. 1, n. 8), chap. III, pp. 162–266.
13 Blakney (cited chap. 7, n. 1), pp. 258–305.
14 Note that by this criterion Erasmus should be seen as a mystic. And why not? See M.A. Screech, *Erasmus: ecstasy and the praise of folly* (London: Duckworth, 1980, repr. Harmondsworth: Penguin, 1988). In developing his ideas about madness, folly, and ecstasy Erasmus is moving, like Eckhart, towards affirming the pure gratuitousness and contingency of life. This liberates us from the anxiety of accountability.

Chapter 9: Happiness

1 See the very early credal confession in *Deuteronomy* 26: 5b–10.
2 S.G.F. Brandon, *The Judgement of the Dead* (London: Weidenfeld and Nicolson, 1967). On this whole subject, see also Graham

Shaw, *God in our Hands* (London: SCM Press, 1987), Part One.

3   Is Michelangelo's Doom-painting in the Sistine Chapel the last major one? For a late Hellfire sermon, see the one described in Joyce's *Portrait of the Artist as a Young Man*.

4   See N.K. Sandars, *The Epic of Gilgamesh* (Harmondsworth: Penguin, revised edn of 1972), chap. 1.

5   For Dogen on this, see Yuho Yakoi, *Zen Master Dogen: an introduction with selected writings* (New York: Weatherhill, 1976), p. 109f., quoting the *Shobo-genzo*, § *Hotsu Bodai-shin*.

6   The Fountain is discussed at more length in my *After All* (London: SCM Press, 1994), and *The Last Philosophy* (London: SCM Press, 1995).

7   The works of the Oxford philosopher D.F. Pears give the best account of these matters. See his *Bertrand Russell and the British Tradition in Philosophy* (London: Collins, 1967); and on Wittgenstein, *The False Prison* (Oxford: Clarendon Press, 2 vols, 1987, 1988).

8   Cited from Mark Rutherford's *Deliverance* (1885). See William Hale White, *The Autobiography of Mark Rutherford and Mark Rutherford's Deliverance* (London: Libris, 1988), pp. xviif., 133f.

9   Chap. 1, above.

10 Mircea Eliade, *From Primitives to Zen* (London: Collins, 1979) chap. II A, gives a range of examples – Maya, Manu, Maori – and doesn't need to mention the more familiar Memphis and Israel.

11 Being facetiously sexist in order to make the point understood, I have commanded my students of both sexes to "Think female! Write male!" They remember that. See chap. 4, n. 8 above. Something very similar is said by Nietzsche.

Chapter 10: Eternity

1   Geoffrey Grigson (ed.), *Poems of John Clare's Madness* (London: Routledge and Kegan Paul, 1949), pp. 133f.

2   For example, ibid., nos 52 and 53, both addressed to Mary. For Clare's religious emotivism, consider the line: "Poets love nature, *and themselves are love*" (my italics); no. 48, on p. 125.

3   The outstanding exponent of this theme is Feuerbach: "God himself is nothing else than undisturbed, uninterrupted feeling, feeling for which there exists no limits, no opposite." *The Essence of Christianity* (1841), Appendix §2.

4   For example, George Pattison, *Agnosis: theology in the void* (London: Macmillan; New York: St Martin's, 1996), citing Eckhart in his

epigraphs on p. v, and also citing Schopenhauer and the author of *The Cloud* on p. 145. But notice that my interpretation of *The Cloud*, and of mysticism generally, differs somewhat from George Pattison's. As I see it the *Cloud* author is a sort of religious Kantian who wants to destroy knowledge in order to liberate faith, which is pure, solar, outpouring, and objectless desire of the heart. Knowledge in religion is always associated with alienation and the exercise of power.

Accordingly, it is in my view a mistake to set the Negative Theology in a dialectical relationship with positive theology (as preceding it, as an internal corrective to it, and so on); for to set the issues up in this way is still to be revolving about the old obsession with *knowledge*, with objective reality and so with metaphysics. The Negative Theology is thus dragged into playing the very game that it is trying to get us out of.

5   Cited from the old Evelyn Underhill edition, *A Book of Contemplation the which is called The Cloud of Unknowing, in the which a Soul is Oned with God* (London: Watkins, 1912).

6   God dwells in thick darkness, I *Kings* 8:12, and also in unapproachable light, I *Timothy* 6:16; "There is in God (some say) / A deep, but dazling darkness": Henry Vaughan, "The Night."

7   Andy Goldsworthy, *Wood* (London: Penguin Viking, 1996), pp. 28f., 80–3.

8   Robert Hughes, *American Visions* (London: BBC, 1997).

9   Translated as *The Order of Things: an archaeology of the human sciences* (London: Tavistock, 1970), pp. 386f.

select bibliography

The list below is restricted to some of the more useful modern works. For a very full bibliography with over 1,000 items, see Bernard McGinn's first volume (1991), cited below. Details of individual works that I quote are given in the notes above, and are not all repeated here.

Cahn, Steven M. and Shatz, David (eds), *Contemporary Philosophy of Religion* (New York and Oxford: Oxford University Press, 1982), Part II.

Caputo, John D., "Mysticism and transgression: Derrida and Meister Eckhart," in Hugh J. Silverman (ed.), *Derrida and Deconstruction*, Continental Philosophy IV (New York and London: Routledge, 1989).

Carter, Robert E. (ed.), *God, the Self and Nothingness: reflection Eastern and Western* (New York: Paragon House, 1990).

Cupitt, Don, *The Time Being* (London: SCM Press, 1992).

Danto, Arthur C., *Mysticism and Morality: oriental thought and moral philosophy* (New York: Columbia University Press, 1987).

de Certeau, Michel, *The Mystic Fable. Volume One: The Sixteenth and Seventeenth Centuries*, translated by Michael B. Smith (Chicago: University of Chicago Press, 1992).

Ellwood, Robert S., *Mysticism and Religion* (Englewood Cliffs, NJ: Prentice Hall, 1980).

Forman, R.K.C. (ed.), *The Problem of Pure Consciousness: mysticism and philosophy* (New York and Oxford: Oxford University Press, 1990).

Garfield, Jay L., *The Fundamental Wisdom of the Middle Way: Nagarjuna's Mulamadhyamakakarika* (New York and Oxford: Oxford University Press, 1995).

Goleman, Daniel, *The Varieties of the Meditative Experience* (London: Rider and Co., 1978).

Huntington, C.W., Jr, with Geshe Namgyal Wangchen, *The Emptiness of Emptiness: an introduction to early Indian madhyamika* (Honolulu: University of Hawaii Press, 1989).

Katz, Steven (ed.), *Mysticism and Philosophical Analysis* (New York: Oxford University Press, 1978).

Katz, Steven (ed.), *Mysticism and Religious Traditions* (New York: Oxford University Press, 1978).

King, Ursula (ed.), *Turning Points in Religious Studies* (Edinburgh: T. and T. Clark, 1990), essays 15, 16.

Kirk, K.E., *The Vision of God: the Christian doctrine of the summum bonum* (London: Longmans, Green, 1931).

Lewis, I.M., *Ecstatic Religion: an anthropological study of spirit possession and shamanism* (Harmondsworth: Penguin, 1971).

McGinn, Bernard, *The Foundations of Mysticism: origins to the fifth century*, Vol. 1 of *The Presence of God: a history of Western Christian mysticism* (London: SCM Press, 1992).

Nicholson, R.A., *Studies in Islamic Mysticism* (Cambridge: Cambridge University Press, 1921, repr. 1967).

Parrinder, Geoffrey, *Mysticism in the World's Religions* (London: Sheldon Press, 1976).

Proudfoot, Wayne, *Religious Experience* (Berkeley: University of California Press, 1985).

Ramanujan, A.K. (ed. and tr.), *Speaking of Siva* (Harmondsworth: Penguin, 1973).

Rist, J.M., *Plotinus: the road to reality* (Cambridge: Cambridge University Press, 1967).

Smith, Margaret, *The Way of the Sufis: the early Christian mystics and the rise of the Sufis* (London: Sheldon Press, 1976).

Stace, W.T., *Mysticism and Philosophy* (New York and London: Macmillan, 1960).

Watts, A.W., *The Way of Zen* (London: Thames and Hudson; New York: Pantheon Books, 1957).

Zaehner, R.C., *Mysticism Sacred and Profane: an inquiry into some varieties of praeternatural experience* (Oxford: Clarendon Press, 1957).

index